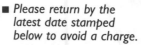

HOME HINTS & TIPS

The new guide to natural, safe and healthy living

ROSAMOND RICHARDSON

A Dorling Kindersley Book

LONDON, NEW YORK, MUNICH, MELBOURNE, and DELHI

To Kay, with thanks and appreciation

Project Editor Bella Pringle **Art Editor** Jane Forster
Senior Editor Jennifer Jones **Managing Editor** Gillian Roberts
Senior Art Editor Karen Sawyer **Art Director** Tracy Killick
Category Publisher Mary-Clare Jerram
DTP Sonia Charbonnier **Production Controller** Joanna Bull

IMPORTANT NOTICE

Every effort has been made to ensure that the information contained in this
book is complete and accurate at the time of printing. However, the
information in this book is liable to change. The ideas, procedures, and
suggestions contained in this book are not intended as a substitute for
consulting the relevant professional. Neither the author nor the publisher
shall be liable or responsible for any loss or damage allegedly arising from
any information or suggestion in this book.

First published in Great Britain in 2003
by Dorling Kindersley Limited
80 Strand, London WC2R ORL
A Penguin Company

2 4 6 8 10 9 7 5 3 1

A CIP catalogue record for this book is available from
The British Library

ISBN 0 7513 3690 4

Colour reproduced in Singapore by Colourscan

Printed and bound in Slovakia by TBB s.r.o.

See our complete catalogue at
www.dk.com

CONTENTS

6 INTRODUCTION

8 HOME BASICS
10 The Natural Home
14 Conserving Water
16 Air Quality

18 SAVING ENERGY
20 Lighting
22 Heat & Insulation
26 Household Appliances
28 Travel

30 DECORATING
& FURNISHING
32 Painting & Decorating
36 Soft Furnishings
40 Synthetic Fabrics
42 Carpets & Natural Flooring

44 CLEANING THE HOME
46 Natural Cleaners
50 Windows, Walls, & Floors
52 The Natural Kitchen
54 The Natural Bathroom
56 Furniture & Ornaments
60 Household Pests

62 WASHING & LAUNDRY
64 Laundry Know-How
66 Natural Stain Removers
70 Washing the Natural Way
72 Drying & Pressing

74 RECYCLING WASTE
76 Reducing Waste
78 What to Recycle?
82 Organic Waste
84 Hazardous Household
Waste
86 Reusing

88 HEALTHY FOOD
90 A Good Diet
92 Organic Food
96 Reading the Label
98 What We Drink
100 Food Suppliers
104 Grow Your Own
106 Preparing Food
108 Storing & Cooking

110 PERSONAL CARE
112 Understanding Labels
114 Skin Care
118 Body Care
120 Hair Care
122 Hand & Foot Care
124 Fragrances

126 NATURAL REMEDIES
128 Common Ailments
130 The Herbal Medicine
Chest
132 Healing Through
Bodywork

134 BABY CARE
136 Feeding Young Children
138 Nappies & Skin Care
140 Clothes, Bedding, & Toys

142 KEEPING PETS
144 Feeding Your Pet
146 Pest Control
148 Pet Health
150 Pet Hygiene

152 WORKING AT HOME
154 Designing a Home Office
158 Creating a Workstation
160 Money Matters

162 Resources
178 Index
186 Glossary
192 Acknowledgments

INTRODUCTION

This book is a practical guide to creating a healthy, safe, and natural home. It shows how, instead of using synthetic and often toxic chemicals, we can change quite easily to using natural substances that are equally effective but have no side effects.

The book is packed with detailed information designed to raise awareness of the effects of our everyday housekeeping on our health and safety, and to show how easy it is to change even long-term habits. It offers straightforward practical advice in the form of hints and tips. Many of these are time-honoured ideas based on readily available materials, while a comprehensive Resources section lists where to find more unusual products. Animal rights, fair trade, and environmental impact are all issues involved in the decisions we make, and these are addressed too.

The book also offers useful tips on reusing and recycling, which play their part in dealing with the issue of what happens to items once we have used them. Everything has to go somewhere, and the planet is fast running out of dumping places. Plastic, for example, does not biodegrade but sits in landfill sites, leaking toxic gases and polluting the water supply. Depositing at sea is no solution, nor is incineration, since it releases toxic fumes.

We leave our "ecological footprints" behind us in the way in which we live our lives as consumers or users. We have choices to make. Buying less, and more thoughtfully, reusing and recycling, using less petrol by cutting down on unnecessary travel or going by bicycle instead, reducing our use of plastic, choosing organic foods and making choices that encourage biodiversity, cutting back on processed foods whose manufacture impacts on the environment, switching to non-toxic cleaning products, and using natural rather than synthetic materials in the home – all these are areas of our lives over which we have control, and even small changes can add up to something significant if we all make them.

This is the new housekeeping.

Rosamond Richardson

HOME BASICS

Many of us have heard of "sick building syndrome" in air-conditioned offices where toxic emissions from the synthetic building fabric affect the air within the structure, but few of us have realized that our homes can be similarly affected – until now, that is. Increasingly, we are becoming aware that health and environmental concerns need to be taken into account at home too. In response to this new awareness, specialist "biological architects" and some environmentally conscious builders are designing houses that are detrimental neither to health nor to the local ecology. They build on carefully selected sites, and use sustainable construction materials from regional sources that do not need to be transported long distances, a process that consumes large amounts of petrochemicals.

CREATING A HEALTHIER HOME

Few of us can go so far as to build new houses for ourselves, and must make the best of the homes we have, built with more conventional construction methods. With a few simple measures – choosing non-toxic finishes and natural furnishings to improve air quality, for example, or changing the way we use energy to conserve natural resources – we can do much to make our homes healthier and more environmentally sound.

Buy reconditioned tools with wooden handles. They will do the job just as well as their plastic-handled equivalents, and will also save you money.

Building materials p11

Wood flooring p12

Conserving water p14

Improving air quality p17

9

THE NATURAL HOME

It is perfectly possible to use construction materials derived from natural resources when building or repairing a house, instead of man-made materials that are based on chemicals and have a heavy impact on the environment. Using wood (from sustainable sources), cellulose, ceramics, metal, or stone is a sound way of ensuring a healthy home.

HOME HEALTH CHECK

An absolutely safe and healthy home is the ideal, but this is difficult to achieve in the real world. If you are moving, you should avoid those properties with a low "health score". If not, there are still ways to make your existing home safer.

● If possible, avoid living in a building close to power lines or mobile phone transmitters. These emit electromagnetic radiation at various frequencies and intensities that may be harmful (*see Resources page 163*). The health implications of EMFs are not proven, but they may be associated with fatigue and short-term memory loss.

● Avoid properties close to busy roads and industrial sites, as these cause air pollution.

● Choose a home built on well-drained land to decrease the risk of damp.

● If buying an older property, have a search done for lead-based paint and lead pipes – lead contaminates the water supply – and asbestos, which is hazardous when disturbed during house repairs.

● Test the gas supply for leaks, and have faulty or old wiring replaced to prevent fire.

● Have your home tested for radon, and take the necessary steps to prevent it entering the building (*see Resources page 163*). Radon, which occurs as a colourless, odourless gas, is a type of natural radiation, and is known to cause lung cancer.

● If your garage is attached to the house, create an airlock between it and the living space, or fit a well-sealed door, to prevent petrol fumes from entering the living quarters.

● Make sure that your home is well insulated to save energy, but not over-insulated, so that clean air can flow freely.

When renovating an old house, have separate boxes for sorting wood, metal, and electrical wires for recycling.

RESTORING & RENOVATING

In old houses, most of the materials used in the original construction will have ceased releasing toxins, but take care if removing old insulation fibres as they can be hazardous.

● Wear a mask if you intend to remove old insulation or pressboard. Foam insulation and mineral-wool fibres, lead in paint, and wood treated with pesticides are all dangerous and may cause respiratory and other health problems. Asbestos is hazardous when disturbed, as it contains microscopic fibres that can be inhaled, causing permanent damage to lungs.

● If an area containing asbestos needs to be repaired or removed, get an expert in to deal with it safely (*see Resources*

page 163). Never handle asbestos yourself, even if it is present in only small quantities.
● Salvage materials to reuse at a later date in the house, or sell them to a reclamation yard: bricks, stones, timber flooring, window frames and beams, tiles and slates are expensive to buy new or secondhand, so remove them carefully and store until they are required. Metals, glass, and thermoplastics can be reused, and so can timber that is still in good condition. Wood that is rotten can be shredded and added to the compost heap (see page 82), along with thatching reeds and paper products used in natural insulation.
● Use recycled materials for your renovations: find a local reclamation yard that stocks old doors, shelving, and masonry that match the style and period of your house.

NEW MATERIALS CHECKLIST

Whether you are building, renovating, or doing a small repair job, check that your choice of new materials meets the following criteria before you buy.

● Non-toxic: many processed construction materials are toxic. Pressed-wood products (see box) are great offenders: opt for solid woods instead.
● Ecologically sound: check that the material has a certificate to verify that it comes from a sustainable source. This will ensure that the manufacturer is not contributing to the pollution of the environment.
● Local: by buying local materials you avoid the pollution caused by transporting them.
● Biodegradable: new paper-based insulation products (see Resources page 163) break down and do not add to landfill sites.

NATURAL BUILDING PRODUCTS

● Clay or lime plaster for walls
● Lime mortar for brickwork
● Rush and lath plaster – especially good for ceiling work
● Gypsum plasterboard for interior walls and ceilings
● Clear silicone for caulking
● Stone, marble, slate, and granite for floors and other surfaces – excellent for kitchens and bathrooms
● Ceramic tiles, brick, concrete, and natural linoleum for flooring
● Copper pipes for plumbing with lead-free soldering and joints
● Solid wood from sustainable sources for carpentry and flooring (see page 12)
● Cellulose-based insulation materials (see page 24)

Linseed oil putty is made from flax seed. Not only does it smell natural, it is a filler that allows wood to breathe.

SUSTAINABLE WOODS

Most people are aware that softwoods come from fast-growing trees, which make well-managed woodland easy to sustain. Buy hardwoods from responsible suppliers, but avoid tropical hardwoods if possible.

ACCEPTABLE SOFTWOODS

The common softwoods used to make low-cost furniture include pine and birch. Check the origin of the wood before purchase and look out for items made of willow – very fast-growing – bamboo, cane, and coconut, all of which are renewable resources.

Pine and larch are pale-coloured softwoods with a light grain. Responsible suppliers will tell you their origin, and whether they have been treated with pesticides and preservatives.

ACCEPTABLE HARDWOODS

● Sustainable hardwoods include alder, apple, aspen, beech, elm, hickory, lime, oak, pear, plane, poplar, European and black walnut, ash, box, cherry, maple, myrtle, and olive.
● Try to buy native hardwoods, from a local supplier, to avoid unnecessary transport.
● Avoid tropical hardwoods such as mahogany, teak, iroko, African walnut, agba, bubinga, ebony, Honduras cedar, Indian laurel, obeche, sapele, tulip-wood, wenge, and zebrano. Felling them depletes the rainforests, and they also need to be transported across vast distances, which is an energy-intensive process.

● Check that hardwood timber is free from toxic pesticides or preservatives.
● Buy recycled timber from reclamation yards.

Maple, walnut, elm, white oak, cherry merbau, and sustainable Rhodesian teak are all hardwoods with a rich colour and distinctive grain, and are available from reputable suppliers.

WOOD TREATMENTS

Many softwood trees, including yew, whitewood, pine, larch, hemlock, and spruce, are treated with chemicals to produce high-yielding crops and, once the wood is milled, it is often treated with a chemical finish. Familiarize yourself with the following toxins used in timber production and, if possible, avoid them. Timber treated with less toxic substances is also available.

● Lindane, an organochloride insecticide, is a suspected carcinogen – it has also had a devastating effect on the world bat population.

● The insecticide dieldrin and the preservatives pentachlorophenol (PCP) and tributyltin oxide (TBTO) are toxic and are now banned for home wood treatments in many countries.

● Polyvinyl chloride (PVC) is used in flooring products and replacement window frames. Some vinyl products may give off chemical fumes.

● Formaldehyde, used as an adhesive in pressed-wood products, is a volatile organic compound (VOC) and may give off vapours at normal room temperature. It can cause irritation to the eyes, nose, and throat, and breathing problems.

● Melamine, a thermoplastic used to coat kitchen units and worktops to make them easy to wipe clean, may also contain formaldehyde residues.

● Insecticides made from synthetic pyrethroid (the active ingredients to look out for on the label is permethrin) are far less toxic, and are more bat-friendly than lindane (see left).

● Timber preservatives based on inorganic borates have low toxicity and low environmental impact. Inorganic borates are also highly effective as remedial and preventative treatments for wet and dry rot. Borax suppresses mould growth and also acts as a fire retardant.

REDUCING TOXIC EMISSIONS FROM WOOD FITTINGS

• Maintain moderate indoor temperatures. For every 5 °C (10 °F) increase in temperature, formaldehyde, used as a wood treatment, doubles the amount of toxins it "off-gases".

• Improve your household ventilation by letting in plenty of fresh air.

• Seal existing pressed-wood surfaces with a non-toxic sealant such as shellac varnish, to prevent toxic resins from giving off fumes.

VARNISHING WITH SHELLAC

Unlike most other wood varnishes, which are made from petrochemicals, shellac is a 100 per cent natural gum derived from "lac", a scale-insect secretion. Use it to varnish wood shelves and other wooden fixtures to create a clear, hardwearing surface. Shellac varnish is also very good for sealing any treated wood surface that you have inherited from a previous homeowner, as it will prevent the wood from emitting any toxic vapours. Shellac varnish is available from most large DIY stores, is quick and easy to apply, smells good, and dries to a matt finish in 2–3 hours.

1 Using fine grade sandpaper or wire wool, gently rub down the painted or plain wood surface.

2 Paint on the shellac varnish in smooth strokes. Leave it to dry for 2–3 hours, then apply a second coat.

CONSERVING WATER

The average homeowner uses between 120 and 200 litres (27 and 44 gallons) of water per day but, by being a little more careful, we can reduce this to 80 litres (18 gallons). Furthermore, sources of water worldwide are becoming increasingly polluted with fertilizers, pesticides, and slurry from agriculture, while sewage, detergents, and toxic chemical residues are poured into the water system. By taking responsibility for our water use and for the ways in which we dispose of liquid toxic waste, we can make a positive contribution to water quality.

To save water, refrigerate filtered water rather than running the cold tap until the water is cold enough to drink.

USING LESS WATER

Water is an increasingly scarce commodity, so reducing water use can make a real difference, especially when you consider that home use accounts for 65 per cent of all consumption. Here are some ideas for saving water in the home and garden.

Spray taps use far less water than steady-flow taps, and they also wash the dirt off fruit and vegetables effectively.

AROUND THE HOME

● Install a water meter to measure your water use. Figures show that people who use meters consume 10–20 per cent less water on average.
● Check for leaks: one drip per second wastes 4 litres (1 gallon) of water per day.
● Instead of a boiler and storage tank, install a combination boiler or instant water heaters. These heat only as much hot water as needed, and so cut down on water use (and save energy).

IN THE KITCHEN

● Wash dishes by hand in a washing-up bowl, not under constant running water.
● Run the dishwasher cycle only when you have a full load, to save water and energy.
● Run your washing machine on full loads only; a full load uses less water than two half-loads, as each cycle uses up to 100 litres (22 gallons).
● When you buy a new washing machine, make sure you get a water-efficient one: this could reduce your water consumption by 5 per cent.
● Always try to use the energy-economy cycle when machine-washing any item.

USING THE TOILET

- Put a water-saving device in your cistern. Water authorities supply these, or you could improvise your own. Fill a bottle with water, replace the cap, and float it in the cistern. This displaces some of the water and reduces the quantity used in each flush. Alternatively, cut a plastic bottle in half, half-fill with pebbles or marbles to weigh it down, and place in the cistern.
- If you have an old-fashioned water closet with a high, suspended tank, do not replace it: these use less water than most modern flush cisterns.
- Install a dual-flush system that uses only a small amount of water for liquid waste and a larger volume for solid waste (*see Resources page 163*).
- If practical, install a low-flush toilet (*see Resources page 163*) that reduces the average flush from 9 litres (2 gallons) to 4 litres (1 gallon).

IN THE BATHROOM

- Turn off the tap when brushing your teeth: running water for 1 minute uses up 10–14 litres (2–3 gallons).
- Take showers rather than baths as they use less water.
- Install a water-saving showerhead (*see Resources page 163*) that fills each droplet with air, giving three times the efficiency of a normal showerhead but saving water at the same time, while also reducing limescale build-up.

WATER TREATMENT PLANTS

Water for domestic use is pumped from rivers, aquifers, and reservoirs to treatment plants where it is filtered, and sterilized with chemicals such as chlorine before it reaches the taps in our homes. Some companies use ultraviolet radiation instead of chlorine to disinfect water supplies, which is more environmentally friendly since it is chemical-free, and the radiation doses are far too low to be a health risk. We can ensure that our drinking water is clean – or as clean as possible – by always filtering tap water (*see page 99*) before we drink it.

IN THE GARDEN

- Be conscientious about reducing the amount of water you use in the garden, especially during the hot summer months: in 30 minutes a garden sprinkler uses as much water as a family of four in a day, or 1000 litres (222 gallons) per hour or 600ml (1 pint) every two seconds.
- Mulch your flowerbeds with compost or bark chippings to avoid moisture loss by evaporation (a mulch will also suppress weeds).
- Consider reducing the area of lawn and having a low-maintenance gravel area instead.
- Install a "greywater bypass" system for channelling used water (from baths, showers, sinks, washing-up, and washing machines) by re-routing your pipes into a discharge tank (*see Resources page 163*). This can be used for watering the garden.
- Install a compost toilet (*see Resources page 163*), which uses no water at all. You can use the resulting compost in the garden.

Collect rainwater in a large water butt so that you can water plants without having to use mains water.

AIR QUALITY

Indoor pollution is a major health concern, especially since many of us now spend more time indoors than out. According to research carried out by the US Environmental Protection Agency, the concentration of toxic compounds can accumulate inside buildings, making them 200–500 times higher than outdoors. If you are concerned, buy a home kit to test levels of pollutants, or call in a professional tester. But above all, keep the house well ventilated: even colds and 'flu will occur less often than in tightly sealed buildings.

AIR POLLUTANTS

The US Environmental Protection Agency has compiled a list of the products that it considers are the worst air pollutants in the home. These are outlined below. They are easily avoided, as effective natural or "soft chemistry" alternatives are available.

AIR FRESHENERS
These synthetic fragrances disguise bad smells by releasing a chemical that coats the nasal passages with a film of oil, or deadens the olfactory nerves.

AEROSOL SPRAYS
Used for hairsprays and insecticides, these emit a fine mist that is easily inhaled, and contain CFCs, which damage the ozone layer. Use pump-action sprays as an alternative.

CLEANING PRODUCTS
Formaldehyde, PVC, acrylics, polyethylene, fluorocarbons, polystyrene, polyester, and polyurethane are present in the contents and packaging of many everyday products.

IMPROVING AIR QUALITY

There are many inexpensive ways of instantly improving the air quality in your home. Here are a few ideas to help you achieve germ- and pollutant-free air.

Heat up a few drops of essential oil such as citronella, and its vapour will scent and freshen the air naturally.

● Decorate and furnish your home with as many natural materials as possible (*see pages 32–43*).
● Make your household a no-smoking zone.
● Open doors and windows to encourage air circulation.
● Avoid overheating your home: the higher the ambient temperature, the greater the "off-gassing" of toxic vapours.
● Air dry-cleaned garments outside before hanging in the wardrobe: perchloroethylene used in the process is a suspected human carcinogen.
● Use safe household plastics made from cellulose fibres.
● Replace smaller plastic items, such as wastepaper bins, with natural fibres such as wicker.
● Limit your use of chemical household products.

Scented geranium leaves or herbs in bowls of dehumidifying water close to radiators act as an air freshener.

ELECTRIC HEATING

Homes heated by radiant electric systems have lower levels of pollution than those heated by other methods. But hot air can dry out the atmosphere, causing sore throats as well as damaging wood furniture and plants. To improve air humidity, place bowls of water close to radiators. This will keep humidity levels at between 30–50 per cent – a level which is best for controlling biological contaminants. Buy a simple hygrometer to check humidity levels in your home (*see Resources page 163*). Keep heating on a constant low temperature. This is cheaper and less energy-intensive than a sudden blast of heat.

GAS HEATING

Gas heaters emit carbon monoxide, nitrogen dioxide, and other combustion pollutants, so make sure that they are well vented. Service gas heaters regularly and place a carbon monoxide indicator sticker next to the heater. If the sticker turns black, have the heater checked.

WOOD FIRES

An open fire indoors can emit benzopyrene, so make sure that it is well vented. Have the chimney regularly swept clean of soot and creosote.

MINIMIZING DAMP

Damp, mould spores, and airborne bacteria are common in poorly ventilated homes. Counteract them by installing extractor fans in kitchens and bathrooms. Cover saucepans while cooking, and open windows to let steam escape.

AIR IONIZERS

Ionizers increase the amount of beneficial negative ions (electrically charged atoms) in the air, counterbalancing the positive ion charge from heating systems and other domestic equipment which can cause lethargy, tiredness, and susceptibility to illness.

The peace lily mops up ammonia, acetone, ethyl acetate, benzene, and formaldehyde from the atmosphere.

HELPFUL HOUSE PLANTS

Certain house plants are good at filtering the surrounding air – spider plants can even remove formaldehyde fumes. Plants also increase oxygen levels, act as humidifiers, and may also be fragrant. The following plants can go a long way to improving the air quality of your home by reducing the vapours released by synthetic chemicals.

Aloe vera (*Aloe vera*)

Bamboo palm
  (*Chamaedorea seifrizii*)

Boston fern
  (*Nephrolepis exaltata*)

Chinese evergreen
  (*Aglaonema crispum*)

Chrysanthemum
  (*Chrysanthemum morifolium*)

Corn plant (*Dracaena fragrans*)

Dracaena (*Dracaena deremensis*)

Dwarf banana (*Musa cavendishii*)

Dwarf date palm
  (*Phoenix roebelenii*)

English ivy (*Hedera helix*)

Gerbera (*Gerbera jamesonii*)

Lady palm (*Rhapis excelsa*)

Peace lily (*Spathiphyllum*)

Philodendron (*Philodendron*)

Rubber plant (*Ficus robusta*)

Schefflera (*Brassaia actinophylla*)

Spider plant (*Chlorophytum comosum*)

Weeping fig (*Ficus benjamina*)

SAVING ENERGY

Maximizing daylight p20

Most of us take our supply of energy for granted and are wasteful without realizing how much we can save just by being careful or by changing old habits. Small gestures, like offering a colleague a lift to work rather than travelling in separate cars, soon add up to significant energy savings.

LIMITED RESOURCES

Fossil fuels provide us with most of our heating, lighting, and transportation needs. In doing so, they release carbon dioxide, which causes health problems and global warming. The good news is that our homes can now be connected to electricity supplies that are based on renewable, clean resources such as wind, wave, and solar power – in fact, it is possible to meet nearly half of an industrial country's electricity needs from pollution-free sources. Houses and flats can also be well insulated to prevent heat loss, but need to be well ventilated too, since over-insulation can trap unwanted smells and toxic gases in the home.

Insulating hot water pipes p25

REDUCING ENERGY CONSUMPTION

This chapter shows you how you can cut down on the amount of energy expended to light and heat the home, and when using household appliances. It also suggests energy-saving adaptations, and puts forward ways to save energy when making a short journey or using the car. Most of these tips require little extra effort and have the positive benefit of reducing household bills.

Low-energy appliances p26

Low-energy bulbs are widely available and fit into regular sockets. They are long-lasting and help to reduce bills.

Energy-saving transport p28

LIGHTING

Maximizing natural light in the house has many advantages, not least the beneficial effect on one's own sense of wellbeing. Ultra-violet rays are "germicidal", which means that they are able to kill off dust mites in carpets and other soft furnishings. This is one of the reasons why it is a good idea to air household items outdoors in the sun. However, too much exposure to sunlight may cause damage to household effects: fabric colours can fade, natural wood surfaces may bleach, and paper lampshades can turn yellow if regularly exposed to direct sun.

NATURAL LIGHT

Just by making the most of the available natural daylight that the orientation of your house has to offer, you can heat and light your home without having to draw on gas, fuel, or electricity supplies.

- Place key work surfaces – in the kitchen and the home office – near windows.
- Install skylights in upper-storey rooms to provide a source of natural light all day long.
- If you have a garden, consider fitting French windows to open out onto the area.
- Fit roll-up blinds or tie-backs on your curtains to allow maximum daylight in.
- Keep window panes and skylights clean.

Diffused natural daylight is provided by a wall of glass bricks which lets light in, saves on electrical lighting bills, and offers privacy from neighbouring homes.

CHOOSING LIGHT BULBS

Something as rudimentary as your choice of light bulb can affect the demands you place on domestic energy supplies. Decide whether you need task or ambient lighting, or perhaps both, depending on the room's function, and then use this information

to help you choose the right light bulb.

INCANDESCENT BULBS
- These offer a steady white light that does not cause eye strain, and give good colour rendition.
- They have a relatively short life expectancy and are expensive in comparison to other bulbs.
- Their large heat output wastes energy, so always switch them off when they are not in use.

HALOGEN BULBS
- These last longer than incandescent bulbs.
- They emit a brilliant white light ideal for task lighting.
- They give off a lot of heat but use less energy than incandescents.

"FULL-SPECTRUM" BULBS
- These are designed to imitate daylight, not always effectively.

- They are usually fluorescent, but choose those without enhanced UV rays; they are more eco-friendly.

FLUORESCENT BULBS
- These are the least energy-intensive of bulbs, using one-fifth of the energy of incandescent bulbs and lasting up to eight times longer.
- They use argon gas and mercury – a highly toxic metal.
- They flicker rapidly, from 100–30,000 times per second, which is stressful, affects the eyes, and causes headaches.
- They require special fittings.

COMPACT FLUORESCENT BULBS
- These are the standard energy-saving bulbs. During its lifetime, each bulb saves 180kg (400lb) of coal and keeps 130kg (290lb) carbon out of the atmosphere.
- They last 10 times longer than incandescent bulbs.
- They are excellent for task lighting.

- Compact fluorescent bulbs can be fitted into regular incandescent light sockets.
- The bulbs last longer if left on for a period rather than being switched on and off.

Dormer windows in the eaves allow natural light to flood in. An anglepoise lamp offers good directional light.

DIMMER SWITCHES

Lighting is important in creating the right atmosphere in a room, and dimmers are the ideal solution if you want to be able to change the light levels and save energy.

Operating dimmer switches reduces the flow of electric current to the light sources and therefore uses less energy. Installing dimmer switches so that you can adjust light levels to just what you need, rather than having brighter lighting than you require, and can save fossil fuels as well as reducing your electricity bill.

Standard light switches can quickly and easily be replaced with a dimmer mechanism by a professional electrician without having to change the wiring.

HEAT & INSULATION

Over 50 per cent of our energy bills goes on hot water and heating. There are ways of regulating and saving heat to reduce this expensive energy load, and simple ways of making the most of solar energy. The following advice includes hints and tips for conserving heat and covers the obvious benefits of turning to solar energy.

CONSERVING HEAT

There are numerous practical ways, all quite simple, of saving on your heating bills. You will also be doing your bit to keep down carbon emissions that pollute the environment: even small changes can have a big impact if everyone makes them!

● Insulate your hot water tank: this can reduce the heat loss by 75 per cent.
● To make the most of rising heat, have your living room upstairs.

● Warm air rises, so if you have high ceilings, design a platform area that will be warm and comfortable, and give you more living space.

SECONDARY GLAZING
● Install secondary glazing, especially in the rooms you use the most (but preferably throughout the house). Up to 23 per cent of heat loss occurs through the gap between poorly fitting frames. The crucial factor in reducing heat loss is creating an air space between panes of glass. Secondary glazing is simple to install.
● If fitting new windows, you may need to check with the local authority that there are no planning restrictions.

LOFT INSULATION
● Make sure that your loft is properly insulated. About 8cm (3in) of insulation material will save around 20 per cent of your heating costs – natural insulation materials, which include recycled paper and vermiculite, are now more widely available (*see Resources page 164*).
● Insulating your loft makes the space colder, so if your hot water tank is in the loft, make sure that you insulate the tank and water pipes to avoid freezing in winter (but do not insulate underneath, so that they receive rising heat from below).
● Draughtstrip and insulate the loft hatch.

A light and airy conservatory kitchen is double-glazed to offer a comfortable, well-insulated family room.

CENTRAL HEATING

● Set your thermostat to 20°C (69°F) when the house is occupied. If you go out for more than two hours, turn the thermostat down to 15°C (60°F).

● Fit a timer switch that turns the heating system on and off automatically to avoid wasting heat on an empty house. Install an up-to-date electronic time switch so that you can change the programme easily whenever your daily routine or the weather changes.

● New central heating systems that run off the mains are cheaper, provide better water pressure, and give you more space because they don't need a large water storage tank.

● Make sure that your radiators produce the right output for the room size and are not overheating it.

● Put shelves over existing radiators to help direct warm air into the room as it rises.

● Turn off radiators in unused rooms, and keep doors closed.

● Underfloor heating radiates heat and is less wasteful than conventional systems.

● Consider other methods of heating such as electric storage heaters or a wood burner.

AIR CONDITIONING

● Air-conditioning systems are very energy-intensive. Consult the manufacturer about energy-saving options, such as thermostatic controls for when you are out at work, or zoning systems to cool only the rooms you are using at any one time.

● Set the system a few degrees higher, to save energy.

● About one third of unwanted heat comes in through the roof. Prevent heat build-up by applying a reflective coating to your roof, or staple reflective foil to the roof rafters (see Resources page 164). Installing louvre windows or roof vents can reduce the temperature in the attic by up to 30 degrees.

● Install ceiling fans or floor-standing fans instead.

Fit thermostatic radiator valves to vary room temperatures as required, and save energy.

● Hang a damp sheet or curtain over a window to catch the breeze and cool the air.

● Keep curtains closed in direct sunlight.

● Plant deciduous trees on the sunny side of your home to shade it. A vine on a trellis serves the same purpose.

HOT WATER SUPPLY

● Attach a thermostat to your hot water cylinder and set it at around 55°C (130°F).

● Insulate the hot water pipes between the boiler and tank.

● Old water heaters are far less energy-efficient than modern ones. Replacing a 15-year-old heater can cut your energy use by up to 20 per cent.

● Instantaneous water heaters provide instant hot water. There is no storage tank to hold hot water, so no energy is wasted in heat loss as water travels along pipework.

SOLAR HEATING

It makes sense to use solar heat: fuel reserves are expendable and fuel pollution causes problems to human health and to the environment. Solar energy is secure, clean, and inexhaustible. Here's how to make the best use of natural sunlight.

• Buy a south-facing house to benefit from natural light.

• Install large windows on the sunny side of the house.

• Heat-absorbent building materials – brick, concrete, stone – will store up heat during the day and release it gradually in cool temperatures.

• Invest in a solar wall: this is a transparent insulation panel attached to a masonry wall that collects solar energy. It heats up the solid wall, which then transmits this heat to the internal wall.

• Install a solar-powered hot water system (see Resources page 164).

• Install solar panels on the roof of your house to capture heat from the sun, which is then stored and used to heat your house or water supply. If well-positioned, you can supply at least 40–50 per cent of your heating from a roof-sized solar collector.

WHY INSULATE?

Heat loss from walls, roofs, windows, and draughts can be greatly reduced by insulation. However, over-insulation can cause indoor air pollution (*see pages 16–17*). So the secret is to reduce heat loss while keeping the house well ventilated. Insulating an existing home may seem expensive, but your property could be eligible for an energy-saving grant. This is worth discussing with your local planning authority. Even if you have to pay for the insulation yourself, the noticeable reduction in household energy bills will soon cover the cost of your initial outlay.

NATURAL INSULATION MATERIALS

Not all insulation products are beneficial to the environment, even though they save energy. Try to avoid insulation products that are polluting in manufacture and are difficult to reclaim, such as polystyrene (a by-product of petroleum), expanded polystyrene (bead board), polyurethane foam, and urea formaldehyde foam (or polyiscyanurate foam). The following natural materials are micro-porous and "breathe", so reducing the risk of condensation and problems caused by damp.

A wide range of 100 per cent natural insulation materials are readily available from hardware outlets.

CELLULOSE FIBRE
Made from recycled newspaper, or recycled jute sacking, cellulose is treated with borax to make it fire-resistant. It is available in shredded paper or fibre-pellet form for loose-fill insulation, or as fibre boards for insulating floors, walls, ceilings, and roofs.

WOOD FIBREBOARD
This is recycled wood, bonded together with its natural resins. It is used for exterior insulation in timber-frame construction, and as boards for floor and wall insulation, and soundproofing.

SHEEP'S WOOL FELT
This acoustic and thermal wool felting is treated with borax to make it fireproof and insect-resistant. It is used to insulate walls, ceilings, and roofs.

HEMP FIBRE
A fast-growing crop, hemp is used to make loose-fill cavity insulation, while a hemp and lime mix is used for insulation fibre boards.

COCONUT FIBRE
This is made into thermal and acoustic insulation board.

MINERAL FIBRES
These include:
● Perlite (from vitreous rock, which comes in the form of enamel-like globules)
● Vermiculite (a natural scale-like mineral based on silicates of aluminium and magnesium)
● Foamed glass (glass in cellular form)

FLAX
This fast-growing crop is made into wadding that is used to insulate ceiling joists and rafters, and also for thermal and acoustic wall and floor insulation.

CORK
Tiles provide excellent, warm floor insulation, but make sure they are not treated with a polyurethane finish.

SYNTHETIC INSULATION MATERIALS

These insulation materials are used in modern house construction, so they may already be present in your home. However, if you are doing your own insulating and have a choice in what you use, try to avoid products that contain any of the following.

● Polyvinyl chloride (PVC) plastic found in double glazing window frames is produced using toxic chemicals. This process creates polluting waste, including dioxins. If PVC is burnt, it also emits dioxins, and the ash may contain heavy metals.

If disposed of in landfill sites, other chemicals found in PVC may leach into the soil.
● Manufactured mineral fibres (MMFs) are known generically as "rockwool" and are used as thermal and acoustic insulators in walls, lofts, and for pipe lagging. Slag wool, stone

wool, mineral wool, and fibreglass all come into this category. Their particles may become airborne during handling and can be highly irritant to the respiratory system. They may cause eye and skin damage, and are suspected carcinogens.

MAKING THE RIGHT CHOICE

The natural insulation material you choose will depend on the area of your home you want to insulate. The following suggestions list the best fibres for the task in hand.

WALLS
● Use cellulose fibre, wood fibre, loose-fill hemp, sheep's wool felt, or vermiculite.

DRAUGHTPROOFING
• Fit a flap over the letterbox, and put covers over keyholes.
• Use stuffed draught-excluders made from remnants of fabric along the bottom of doors.
• Use commercial draught strips for doors (brass "atomic" strip works best).
• Hang thick, lined and interlined curtains over draughty windows and doors.
• Install spring hinges to allow doors to swing shut.
• Fit compression seals in strip form for windows, or wiper seals for sash windows.
• Close the chimney flue when not in use.

● Polystyrene beads, although manufacturing-intensive, are far better than MMFs.
● Effective insulation on external walls include lime plaster render, coats of natural resin, wood cladding, tiles, slates, or pebble dash.
● Line internal walls with thermal boards made from natural materials.

FLOORS
● Wall-to-wall carpeting using natural materials (see pages 42–43) prevents heat loss.
● Use recycled rubber or cork for an insulating underlay.
● Layers of old newspapers under carpet or natural resin linoleum make good natural floor insulators.

LOFTS
● Use vermiculite under the floorboards and in the eaves.
● Cellulose fibre is also very effective in loft spaces.

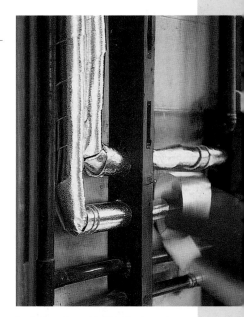

Lag indoor pipes with Climaflex instead of expanded foam pipe sections which, are energy-intensive in manufacture.

● Insulate the loft cold water tank with sheep's wool felt.

HOT WATER TANKS
● Cover with a fitted thermal jacket to reduce heat loss by 75 per cent.
● Insulate hot water pipes with Climaflex, a CFC- and HCFC-free thermoplastic product (see Resources page 164).

HOUSEHOLD APPLIANCES

When buying or replacing household appliances, ask about their energy-efficiency rating. In Europe, the now mandatory Europe Energy Label rates appliances from A–G, and lists electricity consumption standards. Given the improvements that are resulting from these rules, buying a second-hand appliance is probably a false economy in the long-term. Just by upgrading your refrigerator or freezer, for example, harmful carbon dioxide emissions can be greatly reduced.

BUYING APPLIANCES

By making informed choices when we buy various household appliances, we can reduce or minimize the impact these products have on the environment.

- Buy good-quality appliances that will last – and buy only what you really need.
- Choose energy-efficient equipment: hand- or battery-operated gadgets are often just as effective as their electric equivalents. Solar-powered torches, radios, and battery chargers are also available.
- Consider hiring rather than buying a TV and video to reduce the demand for manufacture.
- Buy metal rather than plastic items: plastics release fumes when hot and break more easily.
- Take old appliances to a scrap dealer, not a landfill site.

WASHING MACHINES

- Buy a machine with a hot-fill function (this uses water from the water heater rather than heating its own).
- Front-loading machines use less water and energy than top-loaders.
- Look for a machine that runs on 160 units or less of electricity.
- If possible, set your machine to run on a cheap night tariff.
- Read the manual to get the best out of the machine.
- Excessive vibration can damage working parts, so make sure that your machine stands level on the floor.
- Use a water softener in hard water areas to prevent mineral deposits building up, or add washing soda to your powder.
- Use the correct settings for the size of load and fabrics.
- Always wait until you have a full load before using the machine, or else use the half-load or economy functions.
- Use the lowest possible temperature setting.
- Pre-soaking reduces the amount of washing powder required, and makes a cooler washing cycle possible.

A hand-operated carpet sweeper is brilliant for a quick clean up and only requires your energy to power it.

FRIDGES & FREEZERS

● A cool larder can save on refrigerator space and a smaller refrigerator reduces the quantities of damaging CFCs released into the atmosphere.

Dust the coils at the back of the refrigerator – dust can increase energy consumption by up to 30 per cent.

● Avoid buying a refrigerator that is bigger than you need, and check its energy rating.
● Buy a hydrocarbon-cooled model rather than one using CFCs.
● Insulate the sides of the refrigerator to save energy.
● Keep the refrigerator temperature at 3–9°C (38–48°F), and the freezer at 0– -°5C (32–23°F).
● Avoid leaving the refrigerator door open for longer than necessary, as this allows cold air to escape.
● Leave food to cool before putting it into the refrigerator, and keep it covered.
● Although refrigerators are now very well insulated, try to avoid placing this appliance next to your cooker or boiler: it may have to work harder.
● Connect your fridge-freezer

Defrost the freezer when ice builds up so that it works to maximum efficiency. Full freezers need defrosting less often.

to an energy-saving plug, which works by matching energy to the load required.
● Find out if your local authority offers a recycling service for old appliances.

DISHWASHERS

● Buy the most energy-efficient in terms of amounts of water used and units of electricity used.
● Try not to buy a bigger dishwasher than you really need: the slimline models hold very practical amounts of crockery and cutlery.

● Use the economy cycle for every wash.
● Running a dishwasher on an economy cycle with full loads can use less water than washing by hand.
● Turn off the machine when it reaches the drying cycle to save energy: just open the door.

TV, VCR, & HI-FI

● Keep hi-fi units (CD player, amplifier, tuner, tape player) as close as possible to each other so that they can operate from the same power supply. Separate power supplies will increase your electricity bill.
● Never leave machines on stand-by: it wastes a large amount of energy and is a cause of electrical fires.

● Use battery-powered cordless headphones. Not only do they save energy but they also protect neighbours from unwanted noise.
● Buy a wind-up radio, the ultimate eco-friendly gadget. A mere 25 seconds of winding will give you 30 minutes of playing time, at no cost to yourself or the environment.

AVOIDING EMFs

Electrical equipment gives off EMFs, or electromagnetic frequencies, a type of radiation that may cause health problems. The following tips will reduce your exposure to them:
● Unplug appliances when not in use (they still produce EMFs when switched off).
● Try to do without microwave ovens and electric blankets.
● Sit as far away as possible from televisions, hi-fi systems, and computers.
● Keep beds at least 1.2m (4ft) away from electrical items, such as electric heaters, or electric clocks with electronic number displays.
● Use your mobile phone as little as possible or buy a hands-free earpiece .

TRAVEL

Travelling to work or for pleasure is both energy-intensive and polluting. In terms of toxic fuel emissions, air travel is the most polluting form of transport because aviation fuel is more polluting than petrol. Although many of us still prefer the convenience of the car, travelling by train or bus is a better option because both use far less fuel per passenger. If you do have to go by car, here are some ways to make your journeys more energy-saving.

REDUCING CAR TRAVEL

Travelling by car is often a matter of habit. Try other ways of getting about, and make the most of the car journeys you do take.

● Walk or cycle for short journeys – these activities are good for your health as well as for the environment. A 10 per cent increase in the number of cyclists would lead to a 4 per cent reduction in heart disease. Wearing a pollution mask helps filter out toxic gases.
● Use the train or bus where possible (a double decker bus carries the same number of people as 20 fully occupied cars and takes up one seventh of the road space).
● If you shop by car, do all your shopping in one trip per week, and tie it in with as many other errands as possible.
● Share car journeys with other people.
● Use park-and-ride schemes.

Try to cycle or walk rather than always taking the car. It will improve your wellbeing, both physically and mentally.

BUYING A CAR

The car is here to stay, but by driving well and making informed choices about fuel we can all reduce that impact it makes. The internal combustion engine may soon give way to propane gas, fuel cell, and other technologies, but meanwhile, follow these tips.

● Buy secondhand – it has far less environmental impact than buying new, and it is much cheaper.
● Buy small: usually, small means less polluting. while four-wheel drive increases fuel consumption by 5 per cent.
● Buy a manual-gear car: automatics use more petrol.

● Choose a car with low pollution features like good fuel efficiency, a catalytic converter, and electronic ignition.
● Avoid diesel-fuelled cars. Diesel is far more polluting, containing more than 40 recognized toxic pollutants that cause major health

problems, including cancer, and pollute the environment. If you do have a diesel engine, use biodiesel (untaxed in Europe), which is based on waste food oil – but check first that your car will run on this. Alternatively, try a low-sulphur diesel (*see Resources page 164*), which is a cleaner version of regular diesel.

ENERGY-SAVING DRIVING

The way we drive makes a quantifiable difference to fuel consumption, as well as to wear and tear on the vehicle. Slamming on the brakes, using gear changes to slow down, and revving the engine can increase your bills by 20 per cent.

- Drive more slowly. Speeding along at 113km/h (70mph) can gobble up 30 per cent more petrol than 88km/h (55mph).
- Accelerating gently uses less petrol: drive smoothly.
- Have your car serviced regularly and keep it in good repair.
- Keep tyres correctly inflated: low tyre pressure increases fuel consumption by 1 per cent.
- Remove a roof rack when it is not in use – wind resistance increases fuel consumption.
- Use air conditioning only when necessary – it uses fuel.
- Don't idle the engine when stationary: switch off.
- Drive in the highest gear possible: 60km/h (37mph) in third gear uses 25 per cent more fuel than fifth gear.
- Convert your car to propane gas: conversion is expensive, but the fuel is cheap and less polluting than petrol.
- Use a low-emission unleaded petrol that requires no vehicle modification.

CLEANING THE CAR

It is not strictly necessary to use chemical cleaners on your car: there are some natural alternatives that work just as well. For example, you could use the window cleaner on page 50 to clean all the glass. Here are some other suggestions.

- Baking soda mixed with a little water is excellent for removing insects from headlights, windscreens, and paintwork, and cleans up grease spills.
- Save water: rather than using the hose to wash the car, fill a bucket with warm water and add "soft chemistry" liquid detergent, and clean with a cellulose sponge.
- To clean the windscreen, put soda water into a spray bottle, squirt over the glass, and wipe dry.
- To clean battery terminals, sprinkle baking soda around them, spray with water, and leave for an hour. Sponge off with water and leave to dry.

CAR-CLEANING POLISH

Use this natural homemade preparation to remove surface dirt and give your car a long-lasting shine.

YOU WILL NEED
100g (4oz) soapflakes
  or grated hand soap,
water, to cover
6 drops of jojoba oil
15g (½oz) beeswax

Before mixing the ingredients, dissolve the soapflakes in water overnight. To apply, dab on with a soft cloth, and buff to a shine with a chamois leather.

1 Melt the beeswax and jojoba oil in a bowl over simmering water. Pour the melted wax into the dissolved soap flakes. Beat until the mixture is creamy.

2 Place in a screw-top jar ready for use.

DECORATING & FURNISHING

Decorating a home is an opportunity to create a sanctuary where we can live comfortably in surroundings which give us pleasure. Our choice of materials is key, and natural ones almost always look, feel, and smell better than synthetic products. There is growing concern, too, over the cocktail of chemicals used in the manufacture of paints and textiles. Often there is no list of ingredients on these products, which adds to the difficulty of making an informed choice.

NON-TOXIC PAINTS FOR HOME DECORATING

You can now buy paints that are made without the hazardous substances that harm the air quality in your home. Natural paints offer a smooth, matt finish and are available in a wide colour range.

NATURAL TEXTILES & FABRICS

Bedlinen, upholstery, curtains, and towels in pure linen or cotton, silk and wool are ideal for the natural home. As well as feeling luxurious, they are also practical, resilient fabrics. An "organic" or "untreated" label means that they are derived from fibre crops grown and processed without toxic pesticides, fertilizers, and chemical finishes. Unlike mass-produced fabrics, they are free of vinyl, formaldehyde, and other toxic substances that may cause allergies and sickness. This chapter aims to show you why it makes sense to choose natural paints and fabrics. It describes how and where to apply them, and how to clean and care for them so that they last.

Natural paints are now available in an extensive range of soft colours, and do not "off-gas" during or after application. Pure cottons and linens make durable covers for furniture.

Making milk paint p33

Natural brush cleaner p34

Applying limewash p33

Choosing flooring p42

PAINTING & DECORATING

Although some mainstream manufacturers are now reducing the quantity of chemicals used in house-paints, most commercial paints on the market contain large amounts of hazardous substances. The high levels of toxicity present in paint soon become evident when you begin examining the warnings paint manufacturers are legally obliged to display on tins. Oil-based paints are the worst offenders. They contain toxic volatile organic compounds (VOCs), resins, pigments, and additives such as defoamers (chemicals that break down the foam caused by chemical reactions), deodorizers, stabilizers, and preservatives. Water-based vinyl emulsions contain vinyl resins, which have been linked to various health problems. And although commercial water-based paints may contain low levels of VOCs, their chemical content is still three times higher than that of natural paints.

Organic water-based paints that are free of artificial pigments and chemicals are now available by mail order, so are easily obtainable nationwide.

AVOIDING TOXIC INGREDIENTS

In 1999, a Johns Hopkins University study showed that over 450 toxic chemicals may be present in house-paint. By familiarizing yourself with the dangers associated with chemicals in paints you can make an informed decision about whether to use them in moderation or to opt for a natural alternative.

VOLATILE ORGANIC COMPOUNDS (VOCS)

Most oil-based house-paints contain 40–60 per cent VOCs, a large family of chemical compounds that evaporate easily. These organic solvents are mainly used to help particles in paint to disperse and bind together. Water-based paints contain lower amounts of VOCs (about 10 per cent). VOCs found in paint may include toluene, xylene, and formaldehyde, which are all hazardous chemicals. VOCs "out-gas" at room temperature, and are responsible for the typical new paint odour. The fumes may trigger asthma, allergies, disorders of the nervous system, and 'flu-like symptoms. VOCs also contribute to the formation of ozone at ground level in summer, commonly known as smog.

PAINTING TIPS

If you are using paints that contain VOCs, here are some hints to reduce their impact.
• Ventilate the room during and after applying paint.
• Wear protective clothing, gloves and even goggles to protect your skin and eyes.
• Avoid moving into a newly painted room straight away. Leave it to "off-gas" first for about a week.
• Paint at cooler times of the year to reduce vapour levels.
• Reduce the temperature of your home and keep humidity below 35 per cent to limit the release of toxic chemicals.

NATURAL PAINTS

Paints made from natural raw materials (*see Resources page 165*) have been used successfully for centuries. The principal ingredients are linseed oil, lime from limestone, casein from milk, and natural solvents such as turpentine and/or oils derived from citrus fruits. Chalk and natural pigments make up the remainder. There are now also water-based gloss and satin paints for interior and exterior wood, metal, plaster, and masonry. They may be more expensive, but the benefit is that they contain no fungicides or preservatives. Because they are preservative-free, natural paints do have a limited shelf life: about nine months if unopened. Use the same technique for applying natural paints as you would for any other house-paint; however, some require more drying time because they lack chemical drying agents.

Limewash paint has no smell and is non-toxic. It dries quickly, so apply it with a large, natural bristle brush in broad strokes for a smooth finish.

ADVANTAGES OF NATURAL PAINTS

● Natural paints are micro-porous, so they allow the walls to "breathe". This means blistering and peeling do not occur (as may happen with synthetic paints), nor does moisture accumulate, since it can evaporate naturally.
● The process used to make natural paints produces far less toxic waste than synthetic paint manufacture.
● Natural paints are safe for the environment and are not tested on animals.
● They are less likely to trigger sensitivities and allergies than paints high in chemicals.
● Brushes and rollers can be cleaned with soapy water.
● The packaging is recyclable.
● Although drying time is longer (with the exception of limewash), the paint settles into a smooth, enamel-like coating, free from brushmarks and hairline cracks.

MAKING MILK PAINT

Casein powder, a by-product of milk, can be mixed with water and a small amount of natural pigment to make a wonderfully smooth, matt paint for interior walls.

1 Mix 250g (½lb) casein powder with 340ml (12fl oz water). Whisk to produce a thick batter and stand for 30 minutes.

2 Add a further 125ml (4fl oz) water and whisk to a creamy consistency. Leave to stand for 15 minutes.

3 Mix 50g (2oz) of pigment powder with a little water to make a thin paste. Add to the casein mix, stir, and use.

WORKING WITH PAINT

Paints made from natural ingredients have different properties from ordinary commercial brands. Use these application guidelines to achieve successful results.

● Natural paint is more fluid than other types of paint. When applying it to a ceiling, cut a slit in a sponge and thread it onto the handle of the brush to prevent drips from running down your arm.
● To achieve the smooth, enamel finish characteristic of natural paint, you need to use high-quality bristle brushes with fine ("combed") tips.
● Rollering produces a different finish from brushing, so avoid mixing these two methods of application.
● Spraying with a paint spray gun produces a smooth finish.
● Allow 24 hours for natural paints to dry.
● Although most natural paints are odourless or have a citrus-fruit aroma, you can remove unwanted smells by placing a few slices of onion in a dish of water.

BRUSH-CLEANING PRODUCTS

The most common brush cleaners for oil-based paints are white and methylated spirits, but as these are based on petrochemicals they are best avoided completely. Instead, clean your brushes with solvent-free, water-based products. These have no toxic effects and minimal VOC content (*see Resources page 165*).

DISPOSING OF PAINT

● Local authorities have specific guidelines for the disposal of paint, strippers, and finishes, which are defined as hazardous waste products. Paint waste contains many toxins and heavy metals, including lead, and should not be tipped into a landfill site.
● Keep any leftover paint for retouching paintwork.
● Donate unused paint to local community groups or charitable organizations.

GARDEN USES

● Organic paints are not harmful to plants and contain natural oils and minerals, so any dried-up remains can safely be added to compost.
● Leftover limewash paint can be brushed onto the trunks of fruit trees to deter pests.

NATURAL BRUSH CLEANER

Turpentine, derived from the natural resin of coniferous trees, is an excellent brush cleaner for oil-based paints. It can be rinsed down the sink as it does not harm the environment. All you need is a glass jar, washing-up liquid, and clean water for rinsing.

1 Pour enough turpentine into the jar to cover the bristles. Leave the brush to soak for 20–30 minutes.

2 Clean off any excess paint with lukewarm water and a small amount of "soft chemistry" washing-up liquid.

3 Rinse out the soapy water and paint under a tap. Shake the brush, then dry it flat to keep the bristles straight.

WORKING WITH WALLPAPER

Wallpaper manufacturers often give a vinyl or plastic finish to decorative papers to make them easier to wipe clean. Wallpaper pastes also contain chemical solvents. Some wallpaper manufacturers, however, now produce a range of papers from recycled cotton or paper pulp, as well as clay-coated papers. Water-based wallpaper pastes are also available, and these offer a preferable alternative to chemical solvent-based glues.

AVOIDING CHEMICAL SOLVENTS

Chemical wallpaper strippers are based on caustic soda, which can burn the skin, while products to remove wallpaper glue may contain methylene chloride, which is known to be carcinogenic. Consider the following natural alternatives:

● "Soft chemistry" solvent strippers are available, but may need to be left on overnight to allow time for them to work. Apply a second coat of stripper before peeling off the wallpaper.

● Some wallpapers may peel off dry. If not, follow the technique described below.

NATURAL WALLPAPER STRIPPER

The following step-by-step sequence shows how you can remove wallpaper without the use of chemical solvents. A simple solution of hot water and white vinegar is applied to the paper and left to soak in. This reacts with the wallpaper paste and loosens it, making it much easier to peel off with a scraper. If you wish to paint the walls afterwards, you may need to remove any traces of wallpaper solvent by rubbing gently with sandpaper to create a smooth surface, then wipe down the wall with a damp cloth and leave to dry before redecorating.

1 Using a craft knife, score the wallpaper to be removed.

2 Pour 300ml (½ pint) white vinegar into a bucket of hot water. Brush onto the paper with a wallpaper brush, and leave the solution to penetrate the paper.

3 The vinegar solution reacts with the wallpaper paste and helps to loosen it. This will allow you to gently ease the paper away from the wall surface with a metal scraper.

SOFT FURNISHINGS

Man-made fibres may now dominate the textile market, but natural fabrics – especially those derived from organic sources and coloured with natural dyes – are better for our health and sense of wellbeing, and far gentler on the environment. Although more expensive than synthetic fibres, good-quality natural fabrics are perhaps a better investment in the long term as we are more inclined to take care of them and repair them before throwing them out. To maintain soft furnishings in pristine condition, always read the care label instructions before cleaning, and follow the advice given below.

LINEN

Linen is made from the fibres of the flax plant, and is often sold in its natural, unbleached ivory colour. The plant has few insect predators but, unless organically grown, it may still be treated with some pesticides. In its natural state linen is crisp, cool, and dries quickly. As it may shrink slightly when washed, it is often pre-shrunk. It is vulnerable to mildew but not to moths. Linen and cotton blends are common and often have a chemical anti-wrinkle treatment that may wash out, leaving the fabric limp.

Organic linen is an attractive fabric with a pleasing natural colour and texture.

Iron linen tablecloths on the reverse side of the fabric with a cool iron to prevent shine.

CARING FOR LINEN

- Detergents (*see page 70*) can alter the colour or produce dappling on linen: use "soft chemistry" options on a gentle washing cycle for delicate articles; a hot cycle for bedlinen.
- Never tumble-dry: this wrinkles linen fibres badly, and also uses up energy.
- Use the natural bleaching powers of the sun to dry white bedlinen and tablecloths, but keep dyed linen out of sunlight or it may fade.
- To prevent shine, do not use too hot an iron on linen and iron it on the wrong side. Work around seam lines carefully so that they do not mark the right side of the fabric.
- Fold articles such as tablecloths and sheets in a different way each time they are ironed, to avoid weakening the fibres along the fold line.
- Prolong the life of bedlinen by putting freshly laundered items at the bottom of the pile so that they are all used in turn, with equal frequency.

COTTON

Cotton is a cellulose fibre and its quality is determined by the length of that fibre. Cotton plants are susceptible to attack from pests and diseases, so they are treated with fungicides, herbicides, and pesticides. Cotton manufacture reduces the residue in the yarn itself, but try to buy organically grown cotton that is free of chemicals, and processed without dyes, bleaches, or formaldehyde finishes. Untreated cotton fibre comes in various natural colours, from ivory to light browns. Sheets and towels made from unbleached cream-coloured cotton are increasingly available.

CARING FOR COTTON

● Most cotton furnishing items are machine-washable. Wash knitted cotton throws and cushion covers on a gentle cycle, and dry flat to maintain their shape.
● Bleach white cotton sheets and pillow cases using a "soft chemistry" bleach and dry in the sunshine, to maintain the whiteness of the fabric.
● Try to avoid exposing coloured cotton tablecloths, curtains, and bedspreads to direct sunlight since the dyes may fade unevenly.
● Iron cotton furnishings with a hot iron, unless they have been treated with crease-resistant chemicals, in which case reduce the temperature setting and iron the cotton fabric on the wrong side to prevent shine.

WOOL

Woollen fabric is woven from the shorn fleece of sheep and is one of nature's most comfortable materials, whether in the form of carpets and rugs, cushion covers, throws, or bedcovers. The natural oils in wool keep you dry as well as warm, yet wool is also porous, letting your skin breathe. The fibres can be spun and woven into durable fabrics, making wool practical for upholstery and floor coverings.

CARING FOR WOOLLENS

● Wash according to the care label. Wool shrinks in hot water, but is less likely to do so if mixed with synthetic fibres.
● Washing can cause wool fibres to "pill" (gather into small matted knots): wash cushion covers inside out to protect the outer surface.
● Wool is fairly stain-resistant: liquids penetrate the fibres slowly because of their natural oil (lanolin) content, allowing time to blot up the stain with absorbent kitchen towel.
● Woollen blankets and bedcovers are often treated with toxic chemicals to make them moth-proof. Choose untreated blankets and store with herbal moth-bags (*see page 167*).

Accidental spills on wool can be blotted up quickly with absorbent paper towel. The oily lanolin in the fibres acts as a repellent so that liquid does not immediately soak in.

SILK

Silk fibre comes from the cocoon of the silkworm. A fine, soft, lightweight material, pure silk defies copying by even the most skilful synthetic methods. The fibre is used to make a variety of fabrics, from the finest organza and crêpe de chine to heavier silk velvet or rough-textured raw silk. It can be dyed in a range of colours, but also stains easily. Silks make luxurious curtains, cushion covers, and bedspreads.

CARING FOR SILK

Dry-cleaning is often recommended but as this is a chemical process, a preferable alternative is to wash silk furnishings by hand. Keep them separate from other items because the dye may run, and do not soak them for more than a few minutes to avoid weakening the fibres. Dry out of the sun to prevent fading. Iron on the reverse while still damp, using a cool iron.

Silk furnishings can safely be handwashed using hand-hot water and soapflakes. Smaller items, such as cushion covers, can be washed in a bowl, and larger ones in the bath.

HEMP, JUTE, & RAMIE

Fibres from the inner bark of plants are absorbent and durable, and are becoming increasingly available (*see Resources page 165*). Hemp is quick-growing and produces a fibre that is stronger than cotton. It is used for canvas, furnishings, and rope.

Jute is an inelastic fibre useful for bags and hessian. Ramie, also called China grass, is taken from a stingless nettle. It is blended with cotton for clothes, knitwear, and upholstery to increase durability. Care for these fibres is as for linen (*see page 36*).

BEDDING FIBRES

The absorbency and feel of natural fibres make them ideal for bedding. Synthetic fibres do not "breathe" and so are often uncomfortably hot to sleep in. Polyester sheets may be covered with a formaldehyde finish to make them crease-resistant. Mattresses made from polyurethane foam are often sprayed with fire retardant. Acrylic blankets, polyester-filled pillows, and synthetic pillowcases further add to the chemical content of bedding, which you will be in close contact with during sleep.

HEALTHY SLEEP

Choose a cotton mattress, or an organic cotton, linen, or wool futon. Wool is particularly suitable for bedding because it both insulates and absorbs humidity well – the body produces considerable amounts of moisture during sleep. To protect the mattress from perspiration and soiling, cover it with a natural mattress pad. Also try organic wool- or kapok-filled pillows.

NATURAL BEDCLOTHES

Because they keep you warm while at the same time allowing your skin to breathe, bedclothes made from natural materials (*see Resources page 165*) help to regulate your body temperature while you sleep so that you do not become too hot . Natural fabrics also feel pleasant to the touch.

● Buy organic unbleached cotton, cotton-flannel, muslin, or linen sheets and pillowslips. These soften with repeated washes.
● Try pure silk sheets and pillowslips. Although expensive, these will keep you cool in summer and warm in winter.
● Choose a natural cotton duvet filled with feathers and/or down. These may, however, be plucked from living birds and you may prefer a wool-filled duvet instead. Both types work by trapping warm air in the filling.
● For warm yet lightweight coverings, choose open-weave pure wool blankets, which trap warm air in the weave, or cashmere blankets.
● Organic cotton throws and organic cotton decorative quilts are also available.

Hanging your duvet out to air on a cold morning will kill off dust-mite eggs and guarantee allergy-free bedding.

CARING FOR BEDDING

As we spend at least seven hours every night in bed sleeping, this environment should be as healthy as possible. This is particularly important if you or your children are asthma or allergy sufferers, as dust mites can penetrate the mattress and mattress cover. Keep the bedroom well-ventilated by opening the windows and airing the room daily. The watchpoints below should help you maintain a healthy bedroom.

● Change and launder sheets, pillowslips, and duvet covers once a week.
● Wash pillows regularly. You can handwash pillows in the bath, using soapflakes, and rinse several times. Dry in the sunshine. Air them outside at least once a month.
● Mattress covers or pads are often overlooked. Wash them once a week.
● Turn the mattress regularly to ensure even wear. Air it outside on a sunny day twice a year.
● Clean duvets once or twice a year, preferably using a gentle machine wash rather than dry-cleaning. Give them a good airing outside in cold weather to kill off dust-mite eggs.

Vacuum your mattress when you change your bedlinen to remove dust. If you are asthmatic, protect the mattress with an allergy-free cover that will deter dust-mites.

SYNTHETIC FABRICS

With their easy-care qualities, man-made fibres are undeniably useful for people with busy lifestyles. They are also generally cheaper to buy than most natural fabrics. However, synthetic fabrics and finishes do have one major drawback: they are made from plastics, which are derived from petrochemicals, and they may "off-gas" these chemicals throughout their lifetime. They also release fibres that can cause respiratory problems.

COMMON SYNTHETICS

Synthetic materials, including nylon, polyester, acrylic, acetate, and PVC (polyvinyl chloride), are found in many household furnishings. Viscose rayon is another common synthetic. Although pure rayon is composed of natural ingredients, such as cellulose and wood pulp, viscose rayon – which accounts for about 95 per cent of rayon on the market – is far from natural. Most soft furnishing fabrics also contain PVC and formaldehyde to make them flameproof and resistant to shrinking and creasing.

Before buying new soft furnishings, find out the proportion of synthetic to natural fibres so you can make an informed choice.

A fake fur throw is one of the few examples where synthetic is preferable to natural – not only is fake fur cruelty-free but it is also washable, instead of needing chemical dry-cleaning. Wash it in a mild detergent solution and dry it flat outdoors.

DISADVANTAGES OF SYNTHETIC BEDLINEN

● Synthetic sheets and other bedlinen give off vapours when they warm up against the skin, which may cause sensitive skin to itch.

● They absorb little moisture but also inhibit evaporation, so make the body feel hot and sweaty, especially in summer.
● They retain grease, which

only strong detergents have the power to remove.
● They have static cling, unless treated with strong chemical antistatic agents.

CHECKING FOR FORMALDEHYDE FINISHES

Formaldehyde-resin finishes on furnishing fabrics have a tendency to break down with wear, washing, and ironing. This chemical breakdown has been linked to both minor and severe health problems. The

following watchpoints will alert you to their presence in fabrics:
● Unless otherwise stated, all cotton-polyester blend fabrics have formaldehyde finishes, especially bedlinen because it requires frequent laundering.

● Formaldehyde is used on nylon to render it flameproof.
● Some "pure cotton" fabrics are given a formaldehyde finish for easy care. If labelled "shrink-resistant" or "non-iron", they will have this finish.

FLAME-RETARDANTS

Some synthetic fibres, such as polyester, are designed to be flame-resistant. Other fibres have flame-retardant chemicals, such as TRIS and formaldehyde, added during manufacture. In many countries, the use of flame-retardant chemicals on fabrics is a legal requirement.

FABRIC DYES

Dyes used to colour fabrics are unstable chemicals. They can be released from damp fabrics and absorbed if in contact with the skin. Some fabric dyes such as dichlorobenzidene (used to colour cottons) are carcinogenic and may be present in imported fabrics.

AVOIDING TOXINS

- Wash synthetics before use to remove excess chemicals.
- Choose good-quality soft furnishings that will last longer, or buy second-hand.
- Extend the life of your fabrics by cleaning them carefully.
- Avoid dry-cleaning to reduce chemical emissions in the home (*see page 73*).
- Choose unlined curtains and covers that you can wash by hand rather than dry clean.
- Read fabric labels to check for the dyes used.

CARING FOR SYNTHETICS

The guidelines below explain how to maintain synthetic soft furnishings. Extending the lifespan of an item with good care reduces the amount of synthetic waste going into the environment, as does recycling worn-out items.

- Read the care label. Failure to launder according to instructions may result in a ruined fabric. Too hot a cycle may shrink or even melt a synthetic fabric.
- Man-made fibres seem to retain stains and odours more than natural fibres, so wash items regularly.
- Wash delicate articles by hand (*see page 71*).
- Most synthetics do not absorb water well and retain oils, so they are difficult to get really clean without the use of strong detergents. Try pre-soaking items in water before washing.
- Use a "soft chemistry"

fabric softener to reduce static cling in synthetic fibres.
- Lay knitted acrylic throws flat to dry, so that they retain their shape.
- Most synthetics do not require much ironing. If you have to iron them, however, use a low setting; otherwise the fabric may melt.

▲ **Turn synthetic cushion covers** inside out before washing to protect the fabric and reduce the chance of "pilling".

▶ **To check for colour run,** steam synthetic fabric between two pieces of white cloth to see if the colour comes out.

CARPETS & NATURAL FLOORING

The majority of modern carpets are made from synthetic fibres – typically about 80 per cent nylon and 20 per cent plastic. As many as 120 chemicals may be used in their production, including volatile organic compounds (VOCs) such as toluene and xylene, and the known carcinogen benzene. If there is wool in the carpet, the pesticide permethrin is often added to protect the fibres from moths, and styrene is used to make the synthetic latex backing. The problem with the chemical constituents of carpet is that they may "off-gas" for long periods, polluting the air in the home, while the solvents used to fix natural floorings to a hardboard base are also hazardous. Children and pets are the most likely to suffer the health effects of regular chemical exposure because they are in closer contact with the floor.

New natural flooring materials include coir, sisal, and jute, which offer attractive and hardwearing floor coverings for heavy-traffic areas of the home.

CARPET FACTS

Unfortunately, all carpet fibres attract and accumulate the dust and pollutants brought into the home on shoes and on the paws of pets. Close scientific analysis of carpet pile has shown that it harbours residues of many compounds, including toxic substances from household cleaning products, hair, cigarette smoke particles, and dust mites, all of which are an inevitable part of modern living.

The industrial processes used in carpet manufacture also cause considerable damage to the environment: carpet factories use huge quantities of water, approximately 75 litres (15 gallons) per square metre/yard, deplete petrochemicals, and pollute air and water supplies with waste products.

FITTING CARPETS

● If you decide on carpeting, use carpet tacks to fasten it to the floor. This will avoid the need to fix the carpet in place with a strong chemical adhesive.
● After installation, try to steam-clean a new carpet with water to remove chemical residues present on the surface.
● Leave windows and doors open after laying a new carpet, until the fumes have subsided.

CHOOSING CARPETS & RUGS

Natural flooring materials are not only a healthy choice because they limit toxic emissions – they are an aesthetic one, too, since they look and feel wonderful. Check carefully, though, before choosing. Although a 100 per cent pure wool carpet may seem like a "natural" option, many wool carpets have a latex backing made with styrene, which may "off-gas" for a long time. Bare floors with loose woven wool or cotton rugs, or coir (made from coconut fibres), hemp, jute, sisal, seagrass or even paper matting are perhaps a better, non-toxic solution, particularly if you wish to create an allergy-free home environment. Many beautiful handcrafted floor rugs can also be bought through fair-trade organizations (*see Resources page 165*).

Fasten a wool rug to a natural wood floor with a non-slip felt mat with an adhesive base, to prevent accidents.

HARD FLOOR CHOICES

Wooden floors are a classic choice, and linoleum is making a comeback. Both have a place in the healthy home.

● Hard- or softwood flooring may be made of pine, beech, oak, or maple. New floors should preferably be made from recycled planks or renewable sources of wood. An existing wooden floor can be sanded, but wear a suitable mask to prevent inhalation of the dust from old varnish. Unsealed wood floors can be treated with oil or carnauba wax (*see page 51*), solvent-free varnish, natural stains or paint.

● Linoleum is made in an environmentally responsible way, from linseed oil (a product of flax crops), ground cork, wood, flour, and resins. These are baked slowly at high temperatures and fixed under pressure to a natural jute or hessian backing material. Linoleum is also static-free, and kills off harmful bacteria found on the floor. (It should not be confused with vinyl, or PVC, flooring, which is a synthetic plastic product. This contains phthalates, chemicals used as softeners in PVC, which are released from vinyl flooring into the air; see also page 141. Since small children often like to play on the floor, they are more likely to be exposed to phthalates. Pets are similarly vulnerable.)

Linoleum is soft and warm underfoot and will insulate your home. This 100 per cent natural product is a good solution for those who like the warmth and colour of carpet combined with an easy-to-clean, hard floor surface.

> **TREATING STAINS**
> (*See pages 66–69*)

CLEANING THE HOME

Natural air freshener p49

A clean, chemical-free home is a delight to be in – it looks and feels good and smells wonderful too. To achieve it, it is important to establish well-defined cleaning routines. These in turn will prevent flooring, furniture, and fittings from becoming so dirty that you have to resort to heavy-duty chemical cleaners. (Most modern households in the developed world contain between 15 and 45 litres/3 and 10 gallons of chemically based cleaning materials.) A file divided into sections for different chores acts as a useful reminder for when each of these tasks are due to take place. In your file, you can also include a note of the useful recipes for natural cleaners to be found in this chapter.

KEEPING DIRT OUT

Follow common sense measures to prevent dirt from entering your home in the first place, such as keeping a doormat in front of each exit, and if possible a second mat on the other side. Getting into the habit of removing shoes when you come in from outdoors cuts down on dirt too.

WATER POWER

The best cleaner in the world is water: soaking is one of the most effective ways of removing dirt, whether it be burnt food in pans, smears on glassware, or obstinate marks on hobs or floors. We rely too much on heavy-duty cleaners when milder solutions are perfectly efficient – they are cheaper and less harmful to our health and the environment too.

Multi-surface cleaner p53

Cleaning grouting p51

Chemical-free aids to store in your natural cleaning cupboard include soapflakes, glycerine, and wire wool.

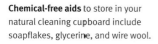

Beeswax furniture polish p56

NATURAL CLEANERS

Cleanliness is vital for a healthy home, but generally we use too many chemical cleaning products and in too great a quantity, and are oblivious to their side-effects. There are time-honoured natural alternatives that are just as effective, do not have such a harmful impact on our health or the environment, and will leave your home smelling delightfully fresh and fragrant – so clear out all your old household cleaners and start anew with the natural alternatives.

SOFT CHEMISTRY

Some manufacturers have devised alternatives to chemical cleaning products based on sustainable vegetable sources. These are known as "soft chemistry" products. They are not tested on animals, are packaged in recyclable materials and, unlike most commercial brands, contain no additives or detergents. In addition, high-street chemists now stock low-allergy cleaning products. These contain no additives or irritants and fewer pollutants (*see Resources page 166*).

CHEMICAL CLEAR-OUT

All these chemical cleaning products can be replaced with safer "soft chemistry" or natural alternatives:

De-greasing cleaners for sinks and baths
Multi-surface cleaners
Washing-up liquid
Dishwasher powders, liquids, or tablets
Toilet cleaners
Floor cleaners
Polishes
Window cleaners
Disinfectants and bleaches
Metal cleaners and scourers
Air fresheners

HOMEMADE CLEANERS

In addition to the "soft chemistry" options that you can buy, you can easily make your own natural household cleaners. These have several advantages: the ingredients are easy to obtain, inexpensive, and have no damaging effect on the environment; they contain no additives, so are unlikely to cause allergic reactions; they are not tested on animals; and they come in recyclable packaging. A list of ingredients and their uses appears opposite.

Fresh lemon, blocks of beeswax, white vinegar, liquid soap, washing soda, baking soda, table salt, and essential oils are some of the key ingredients for a completely natural cleaning kit.

PURE SOAP

Hot water and plain soapflakes with a little washing soda will perform most cleaning jobs. It sounds simple – and it works.

BAKING SODA

A naturally occurring mineral, baking soda (bicarbonate of soda) is a versatile cleaner. It has an infinite number of other household uses. Buy in bulk from the chemist.

TABLE SALT

Salt is a mild disinfectant and makes a gently abrasive scouring powder.

WHITE VINEGAR

The acetic acid in white vinegar cuts through dirt brilliantly. You can use it to clean glass and tiles and to remove tea stains on cups and teapots. Mixed with salt or baking soda, it will polish up brass and copper.

LEMON JUICE

Citric acid is one of nature's great cleaners. Versatile, safe, and fragrant, it cleans fantastically well.

WASHING SODA

Washing soda (sodium carbonate) is a natural water softener and cuts through grease, making it an effective heavy-duty cleaner for painted walls, hard floors, and kitchen surfaces. It is an entirely natural product, and has no negative impact on health or the environment.

BORAX

Also known as sodium tetraborate decahydrate, this is a naturally occurring mineral and may be used in small amounts for removing stains, mildew, and odours. However, it contains the element "boron", which does not biodegrade, and consequently should only be used sparingly.

ESSENTIAL OILS

Tea tree, citrus, thyme, sage, and eucalyptus oils all have disinfectant properties and can be added to any of the natural cleaners above to introduce fragrance. Be sure to buy high-quality, unadulterated oils, and store them in a cool, dark place. Grapefruit seed extract also acts as a disinfectant.

THE NATURAL CLEANING CUPBOARD

Your natural cleaning cupboard should contain the following key ingredients:

Pure soap flakes
Liquid soap (no additives)
Baking soda
Table salt
White vinegar
Washing soda
Borax
Beeswax polish (*see page 57 for recipe*)
Steel wool
Bristle brush
Cellulose sponges
Lemon juice

Bristle scrubbing brushes, wire wool, and linen scree cloths make useful and long-lasting cleaning tools, in preference to synthetic sponges and plastic brushes with nylon bristles.

CLEANING TOOLS

Use old garments and sheets to make rags for your household cleaning rather than buying synthetic ones. When choosing sponges, it is better to purchase the cellulose type (the kind used for cleaning the car) rather than plastic. To get maximum use from each sponge, you can cut it into smaller pieces. Instead of buying treated steel-wool pads, buy varying grades of wire wool and make your own scourer. Use a wooden bristle brush for washing up rather than a plastic brush with nylon bristles.

AVOIDING HOUSEHOLD CHEMICALS

Cleaning the "easy" way with heavy-duty chemicals may not bring the harmony and sweetness to your life that manufacturers would have you believe. Fewer than one quarter of the 70,000 chemicals used in cleaning products and toiletries have been fully tested for safety, and substances classified as hazardous waste are found in many common cleaning fluids.

DETERGENTS

Pure soap – our oldest natural and biodegradable washing agent – is only effective in soft water. So industrial chemists have devised detergents that can cut through dirt but which, when they leach into the water supply, harm living organisms. Most common brands of washing-up liquid and dishwasher products contain detergents derived from crude oil, a limited resource, making these detergents not only a harmful but also an unsustainable option.

CHLORINE

Most dishwasher detergents contain chlorine, a disinfectant, in its dry form. This releases toxic fumes into the kitchen, which can cause headaches, burning eyes, and breathing difficulties. Residues can adhere to the dishes and can leach into the food.

PHOSPHATES

Phosphates (salt of phosphoric acid) act as a water softener and have been added to cleaning products since the 1940s. They may be found in wool-washing agents, multi-purpose cleaners, dishwasher powders, and scouring cleaners. Phosphates are responsible for excessive growth of algae in water systems.

BLEACHES

Most household bleaches are based on sodium hypochlorite, which has a known effect on hormone levels. Bleached toilet paper, kitchen towels, and facial tissues contain residues of toxic dioxins and brighteners.

DISINFECTANTS

These synthetic germ-killers, used in toilet cleaners, contain volatile chemicals, and the fumes they give off can be dangerous to inhale. They can damage the kidneys, liver, lungs, pancreas, and spleen, and interfere with the central nervous system.

READ THE LABEL

Most cleaning and washing products list their ingredients. They may include surfactants, enzymes, phosphates, bleach, solvents (with a warning about solvent abuse), and perfumes. Many contain warnings: that they may release dangerous gases (chlorine); that they are irritants to skin and eyes; and that, if swallowed, immediate medical advice is required. If a cleaning product contains these substances, try to avoid it. Use the natural alternatives on pages 46–47 or buy "soft chemistry" options instead.

PRODUCT FACTS

- The colourings that are added to most cleaning materials are synthetic, and contain heavy metals that damage the environment.
- Sulphates are used in cleaning materials. These are salts that make freshwater rivers brackish and cause corrosion in waste-water treatment plants.
- Synthetic fragrances are based on petrochemicals and can cause allergic reactions.
- Products may be preserved with formaldehyde, known for its allergenic properties.

SAFETY FIRST
All cleaning materials, natural and otherwise, must be kept out of the reach of children.

THE FRAGRANT HOME

Keeping your home fresh and sweet-smelling not only makes it a pleasant environment to live in but can also be beneficial psychologically, calming or uplifting the spirits.

ELIMINATING ODOURS

● Air your home daily by opening the windows.
● Install extractor fans in the kitchen and/or bathroom to remove air laden with moisture.
● Keep your house warm and dry to prevent damp.
● Empty rubbish bins frequently, and sprinkle baking soda into the refuse bag.

HOMEMADE AIR FRESHENER

To eliminate bad odours, create this simple natural air freshener with water and essential oils – lemon and cedarwood are both excellent. Not only can this air-freshener be custom-made with your own favourite fragrance but it will not have a harmful impact on the environment.

YOU WILL NEED:
115ml (4fl oz) water
10 drops of essential oil (neroli is a favourite of mine)

HOMEMADE POT-POURRI

To make your own pot-pourri, use the leaves from dried herbs or flower petals. Choose from peppermint, sage, pine, thyme, lemon verbena, bay leaves, rosemary, bergamot, rose geranium, lemon-scented geranium, scented roses, and lavender. Mix with ground cinnamon or cloves and a sprinkling of ground orris root (a natural preservative), and put in a bowl. Gently toss the pot-pourri from time to time to release the fragrance. As it loses its scent, revive it by sprinkling with a few drops of essential oil.

1 Fill a spray bottle with water and then add the drops of essential oil. Replace the top and shake.

2 A few squirts aimed upwards into the air will make your room fragrant and eliminate pungent odours.

WINDOWS, WALLS, & FLOORS

Proprietary products designed to clean windows, walls, and floors often contain synthetic perfumes that are made up of numerous – and often untested – chemicals. Some carpet cleaners may contain the solvent perchloroethylene, a suspected carcinogen, and naphthalene, a toxic insect repellent. You can look after your health – and your money too – by opting for the following natural cleaning alternatives in your home.

CLEANING WINDOWS

There is no need to rely on chemical sprays to keep windows clean. Instead, use the following tried-and-tested natural methods.

- An effective window cleaner can be made from 1 part white vinegar to 1 part water, with the addition of a few drops of liquid soap.
- To make it easier to see streaks when cleaning glass, use up-and-down strokes on one side and side-to-side strokes on the other.
- Remove the waxy deposit left by commercial window cleaners with a little washing soda solution (2 tablespoons to 600ml/1 pint water).
- If you have a plastic window, do not use a cleaner containing ammonia – it will leave the surface permanently cloudy. Use a handful of pure soapflakes mixed with 1 tablespoon of washing soda and 600ml (1 pint) warm water.
- To clean slatted blinds, take crusts of fresh bread and hold the crusts around each slat as you run them along its length.

For sparkling windows, rub the glass with a sheet of crumpled newspaper and a spray solution of equal parts white vinegar and water, with a few drops of liquid soap added to it.

CLEANING WALLS

Vacuuming will keep painted or papered walls generally free of dirt. For more thorough cleaning, try the following remedies. Unlike chemical products that are designed for spot-cleaning walls only, these can be applied to the entire surface.

- Spot-clean matt, water-based emulsion with a paste of baking soda (*see page 52*). This will remove furniture scuffs, crayon or ink marks, grease spots, and other stains. Leave on for 10 minutes, then wipe off with a damp cloth.
- Clean satin finishes and gloss with a solution of 115ml (4fl oz) white vinegar and 25g (1oz) washing soda mixed with 600ml (1 pint) water.
- For grease marks on wallpaper, cover the spot with blotting or kitchen paper and apply a warm iron so that the paper absorbs the grease.

CLEANING HARD FLOORS

Natural hard flooring, such as wood or tile, is a beautiful surface and one that is easy to keep fairly clean simply with regular sweeping. Untreated wood needs care, including nourishing with wax. Here are some of my tips for natural floor care.

WOOD
● For unsealed floors, apply raw linseed oil on a soft cloth, allow it to sink in, then mop with a little more oil until a shine develops.
● Hard carnauba wax is nourishing for untreated wood floors and brings up a good sheen on the surface.
● Sealed wooden floors need regular sweeping and occasional wiping with a damp cloth or sponge. Wax occasionally to improve the shine.

LINOLEUM
● Mop with a weak solution of a "soft chemistry" cleaner, or my all-purpose surface cleaner (*see page 53*).
● Polish linoleum floor tiles with carnauba wax when they start to lose their lustre.
● Rub off scuff marks with neat turpentine and fine steel wool. Wipe clean with a damp cloth.

TILES
● Cleaning unglazed and terracotta floor tiles with soap makes them go cloudy. Use a 50:50 solution of water and white vinegar.

Clean grouting between floor tiles with baking soda and water on an old toothbrush. Work the baking soda paste into the grout, then rinse off.

● Wipe down glazed wall and floor tiles with baking soda on a damp sponge.
● Remove hardwater spots with white vinegar.
● After cleaning, polish tiles with a soft towel.

STONE
● Never use soap on stone floors. It cannot be absorbed and makes them slippery. Clean instead with a solution of 1 litre (1¾ pints) water to 2 tablespoons of washing soda powder.

MARBLE
● Clean with my all-purpose surface cleaner (*see page 53*). Never use detergent.

CARPET CARE

With a handful of simple ingredients, you can keep your carpets clean without resorting to chemicals. Baking soda is particularly effective, removing grease, dirt, smells, and even pet stains from both natural and synthetic carpets.

● To remove general stains, mix 1 part "soft chemistry" washing-up liquid with 4 parts boiling water. When cool, whip to a foam. Sponge on, then wipe off with a damp cloth.
● For pet or urine stains, apply baking soda or a solution of 3 tablespoons vinegar and 1 tablespoon liquid soap. Leave to work for 15 minutes, then vacuum or rinse.
● Heavy grease or oil stains that resist the baking soda treatment can be cleaned in the same way with cornstarch.
● Steam-clean your carpets using just plain water.

To remove spot marks, sprinkle the area with baking soda. Leave to absorb the stain and then vacuum up.

THE NATURAL KITCHEN

Fresh lemon juice, baking soda, white vinegar, and salt can all be used as natural cleaners as they have cleansing, scouring, and antiseptic properties. They are just as effective as proprietary products that use strong chemicals, and are a lot cheaper. For washing dishes, use a "soft chemistry" washing-up liquid (*see Resources page 166*).

GENERAL CLEANING & CARE

Here are my favoured, environmentally sound methods for cleaning kitchen surfaces and equipment, and maintaining them in good condition. Some of them use the two natural cleaning agents that I have given recipes for: a baking soda paste and an all-purpose surface cleaner.

KITCHEN FLOORS
● To remove grease from cork, ceramic, wood, or stone tiles, use the all-purpose surface cleaner (*see page 53*).
● Sprinkle heavier grease marks with baking soda, leave for 30 minutes, then rub clean.

KITCHEN SURFACES
● Scrub dirty or odorous wooden surfaces, such as

chopping boards, with the juice of half a lemon mixed with 1 tablespoon of table salt. Alternatively, use the baking-soda-paste recipe below.

SINKS
● Clean out the sink with a solution of 25g (1oz) table salt to 300ml (½ pint) water. Salt is a disinfectant and an abrasive.
● A cut lemon removes tea

stains – just rub the cut surface over the stained area.

POTS & PANS
● Rub in baking soda paste (*below*) with a damp cloth or an abrasive pad, then rinse off.
● For burnt pans, sprinkle a thin layer of baking soda into the pan and add boiling water to cover it. Leave overnight, then scour with wire wool.

WATER SOFTENERS
● If you have hard water, add a small handful of baking soda to your washing-up water as a natural softener.
● Instead of using commercial powder in your dishwasher, make up your own using 2 teaspoons each of borax and baking soda.
● Add 2 tablespoons of baking soda to the dishwasher salt compartment to eliminate hardwater streaks.

BAKING SODA PASTE

Baking soda is one of the most useful natural products to keep in your kitchen. It can be put to many different uses, from deodorizing refrigerators and rubbish bins to removing stains. As an all-purpose surface cleaner, baking soda paste is unbeatable. It is non-abrasive, so it can be used to clean chrome and aluminium surfaces, pots and pans, and fridge interiors. Rub on the paste with a soft cloth and buff to a brilliant sheen.

1 Dissolve 4 tablespoons of baking soda in 4 tablespoons of water.

2 Using a soft cloth, rub the paste onto the surface to be cleaned. Wipe off with a clean cloth and buff to a shine.

ALL-PURPOSE SURFACE CLEANER

This cleaner removes grease and dirt, smells beautifully fresh, is cheap and non-toxic, and will keep indefinitely. Use it on stainless-steel sinks and draining boards, tiled and wooden surfaces, and plastic finishes (such as telephones).

YOU WILL NEED:
600ml (1 pint) white vinegar
300ml (½ pint) water
20–30 drops eucalyptus oil

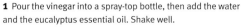

1 Pour the vinegar into a spray-top bottle, then add the water and the eucalyptus essential oil. Shake well.

2 Pour a little of the mixture onto a soft, damp cloth and rub over the surface to be cleaned. There is no need to rinse.

KEEPING APPLIANCES CLEAN

It is important to use the correct non-abrasive cleaner on kitchen appliances as their specialist surfaces are often easily scratched and damaged. Here are my tips for maintaining naturally clean and hygienic kitchen appliances.

REFRIGERATORS
● Clean the inside of the fridge with baking soda paste (*see opposite*). The paste will also work to eliminate any stale fridge odours.
● Charcoal absorbs smells inside fridges; so does cat litter. Fill a dish and leave in the fridge for a day.
● Wipe the door clean with a damp cloth. Use baking soda paste for obstinate marks.

WASHING MACHINES
● Keep your machine clean by running it empty on a hot wash with 60ml (2fl oz) white vinegar in the detergent drawer. Do this every 20 washes.
● Clean out the detergent compartment regularly: remove it carefully, soak it, then scrub clean any residues that may cause blocking.

KETTLES
● To de-scale your kettle, empty, and pour white vinegar over the element. Leave for 1 hour. Rinse with cold water. Pour fresh water into the kettle to cover the element. Boil it, then throw this water away.

OVENS
● To clean the interior of the oven, rub with wet wire wool, then sprinkle baking soda over the dirty surfaces and rub clean with a damp cloth.

MICROWAVES
● To clean and deodorize your microwave, mix 115ml (4fl oz) water with 2 teaspoons of baking soda in a microwave-safe bowl. Place the mixture in the microwave, turn to High (100% power), and run for 2 minutes. Remove the bowl and wipe the oven clean.

THE NATURAL BATHROOM

Rub lemon juice around drainage hole to remove grease and limescale.

The bathroom is one room in the home where it may seem necessary and even justifiable to use heavy-duty chemicals. It is reassuring to know, then, that natural cleaners are equally effective. They are also less abrasive, so they will not scratch enamel surfaces and are kinder to hands.

BATHS, BASINS, & SHOWERS

Most of the cleaners here are natural homemade products, although there are "soft chemistry" options that you can buy. The tools you use are also important. For example, instead of an abrasive scourer to clean a very dirty bath, why not use a bristle brush? For hard-to-reach areas behind taps, an old toothbrush comes in handy.

BATHROOM SURFACES

● Use a baking soda paste (*see page 52*) to clean sinks, baths, toilet surfaces, and taps. Rub persistent dirty marks with a cut lemon.

● Rub stubborn stains on sinks and baths with turpentine oil. Rinse with hot water mixed with a little "soft chemistry" washing-up liquid.

● To loosen dirt on bath enamel, pour "soft chemistry" washing-up liquid into the bath as it is running out, then rinse and brush clean.

DRAINAGE HOLES & TAPS

● Clean drainage holes by rubbing with a cut lemon.
● For brown stains caused by dripping taps, rub with a mixture of 25g (1oz) salt to 150ml (¼ pint) white vinegar.
● Brown staining also responds well to a paste of cream of tartar, made in the same way as baking soda paste (*see page 52*).
● Remove hard-water deposits

from chrome fittings with a salt and vinegar mix (*see left*).
● Remove limescale on taps with a soft cloth dipped in white vinegar.
● Scrub away rust and grime around tap fittings with an old toothbrush coated with a mixture of 1 teaspoon salt to 1 tablespoon lemon juice.
● A little toothpaste on a damp cloth cleans up chrome taps.

SHOWERHEADS & CURTAINS

● Sponge shower curtains with water and baking soda.
● For showerheads clogged with limescale, soak the showerhead overnight in neat white vinegar.

● Wipe hardwater deposits on glass or plastic shower doors with neat white vinegar. Leave for 10 minutes before rinsing off and buffing to a shine with a soft cloth.

Use a darning needle to unblock the holes in a showerhead, then rinse out the head with white vinegar.

TOILET TREATMENTS

When it comes to toilet cleaning, most people feel tempted to make liberal use of strong chemicals, such as bleach, in order to disinfect the area thoroughly. But, as elsewhere in the bathroom, there are "soft chemistry" and natural alternatives which do the same job but without the same potential for environmental harm.

● To clean the pan, pour 150ml (¼ pint) neat white vinegar into it and brush before flushing.
● Disinfect the pan with a solution of 10 drops of tea tree oil in 115ml (4fl oz) of water. Leave it in the pan until the next flush.
● Wipe the toilet seat with all-purpose surface cleaner (*see page 53*).
● For hardwater deposits, apply a mixture of 50g (2oz) borax powder and 300ml (½ pint) white vinegar and leave for 2–3 hours in the pan before flushing the toilet.

TOP TIP

Lighting a match in the toilet after use eliminates bad smells – simple but miraculous!

CLEARING DRAINS

Prevention is the best strategy here – try to limit the waste matter going into your drains in the first place. Chrome drain-strainers placed over plugholes work well.

● To keep drains clear, you can use a handful of baking or washing soda mixed with 115ml (4fl oz) white vinegar (this is a stronger solution than using salt) and simply pour it down the drain and leave to work.
● If your drains become clogged, avoid using a strong drain cleaner, such as caustic soda. Instead, unblock them with a hand-plunger (available from hardware stores).
● "Soft chemistry" options are also available.

MOULD & MILDEW

Bathrooms are humid environments and are particularly prone to mould and mildew. If these are persistent problems, ensure that air circulates near the source of the trouble, and that the area is kept warm and dry.

● Borax prevents mould and mildew from developing. Make a solution of 50g (2oz) borax to 300ml (½ pint) white vinegar and apply with a cloth, or put into a spray bottle to apply to damp walls. Leave for 30 minutes or more before wiping off.
● Spray problem areas with neat white vinegar, leave for 30 minutes, then wipe off.
● Dry portable items in the sun after treating.

Flush boiling water and a handful of salt down blocked or foul-smelling drains instead of resorting to bleach.

CARING FOR MARBLE

To protect marble bathroom surfaces, blot stains with paper towels, then flush with cold water until the stain disappears. Slight surface scratches may be rubbed off with very fine wire wool.

FURNITURE & ORNAMENTS

Most furniture can be cleaned quite simply and naturally and does not need heavy-duty cleaners or polishes. Although they are effective at masking wear-and-tear and scratch marks, synthetic chemical wood polishes give off toxic fumes, and are not particularly good for furniture. They produce a milky finish that some find attractive, but I would always opt for the original beauty of the wood, which is better maintained using natural cleaning products. Brass and copperware, silver and pewter, glass and china, and other delicates need especially careful cleaning – the better they are cared for, the longer they will last.

Using a soft cloth, polish wooden furniture with natural beeswax polish (*see recipe opposite*).

WOOD & BAMBOO

Wood is an absorbent material that benefits greatly from careful treatment, as do more fragile fibres such as wicker and bamboo.

CANE, RATTAN, & BAMBOO

These materials are porous, so furniture made from them sometimes has a protective coating. It should be dusted regularly or cleaned with a damp cloth. You can wash it occasionally with soapy warm water, but never soak cane, rattan, or bamboo, since this weakens the pliant fibres.

If possible, air-dry the furniture in the sun and a light breeze, but don't leave it too long once dry – it can become brittle in the heat.

CARING FOR WOODEN FURNITURE

- Use a beeswax polish to nourish wooden furniture and maintain its shine.
- Use coasters on polished surfaces to protect them from heatmarks and scratching.
- Mop up spills on wood immediately.
- If the surface becomes watermarked, polish with a slightly darker-coloured wax, or touch up with artists' oil paints. Then polish frequently until the mark fades.
- Treat scratches in the same way as watermarks.
- If you are using liquid polish, use a pump-action dispenser. Never use aerosol sprays, since they contain CFCs (chlorofluorocarbons), which damage the ozone layer.

SURPLUS POLISH

Mix 2 tablespoons white vinegar and 2 tablespoons water and use to remove a build-up of polish. Rub off at once. You can also use it to remove stubborn fingermarks.

BEESWAX POLISH

Here is my own recipe for an effective and non-toxic polish. The polish will keep indefinitely.

YOU WILL NEED:
75g (3oz) pure beeswax
150ml (¼ pint) turpentine oil
10 drops of lavender oil

1 Grate the beeswax into a bowl and place over a saucepan of warm water.

2 Stir until the wax melts. Add the turpentine oil, and stir thoroughly.

3 Pour into a tin with a sealed lid. Stir in oil, leave to cool, and replace the lid.

METAL FURNITURE & FITTINGS

Metal items must be cleaned regularly or they will tarnish. A tarnished surface is much harder to clean than a dirty one, but there are ways of restoring natural shine.

BRASS & COPPER
● For a homemade polish that will bring a shine to brass and copper, mix 3 tablespoons lemon juice or white vinegar with 1 tablespoon baking soda. Rub on, and buff to a sheen.
● Immerse deeply tarnished articles in hot vinegar mixed with 1–2 tablespoons salt. As soon as a shine appears, rinse very thoroughly. Don't leave items too long in this solution, or new staining may occur.
● Intricate brass and copper objects can be rubbed with the cut side of a lemon, which can penetrate the metal detail without leaving the powdery traces caused by some proprietary chemical cleaners. When clean and shiny, rub dry with a soft chamois leather.

● When polishing brass fittings on wooden furniture, you need to be careful not to let your cleaning product mark the surrounding wood. Make a paper "mask" by cutting a hole to the exact size and shape of the metal to protect the wood as you polish the fittings.

PEWTER
● Pewter tarnishes easily when it comes into contact with strong chemicals: wash it in warm, soapy (detergent-free) water and polish dry to its lovely dull sheen.
● Never drink fruit drinks or wine from pewter mugs because the acid in these fluids will penetrate the metal and the drinks will take on a metallic taste.

CHROME
● Clean chrome with a solution of 1 tablespoon ammonia to 600ml (1 pint) of water. (This is especially good for greasy car chrome.)

STEEL
● To clean steel knives, dip in diluted lemon juice and vigorously rub off stains with a steel wool pad.

IRON
● Wipe rusted ironwork with a damp cloth, scrub with wire wool, and dry, then oil lightly with machine oil to prevent further rusting.
● Wash cast-iron articles by hand, and dry. Rub with a thin coating of cooking oil to prevent the iron from rusting.

SILVER

The beautiful sheen of silver requires thoughtful cleaning. Never put silver in the dishwasher: it is a soft metal that scratches and damages easily, and can become tarnished by other metals. Always wash silver items by hand with a mild soap (no detergent) and water.

When cleaning silver plate, do not rub too vigorously because the coating of silver is thin and will wear through. Black stains left by egg yolk can be rubbed with the cut side of a lemon, rinsed, and polished dry.

If you are using a proprietary cleaner on intricate silverware, use a soft-bristle toothbrush to remove the residue from the detail. Store silver by wrapping it in soft cloths to prevent it from tarnishing while not in use. Keep it dry.

CLEANING SILVER THE NATURAL WAY

The following method of cleaning silverware is simplicity itself, and involves none of the petrochemicals found in proprietary cleaners.

It can be used to clean any silver objects, as long as they do not have cemented-on parts and are small enough to be submerged in a pan of water.

1 Dip the article into simmering water containing a piece of aluminium foil and 2 teaspoons of washing soda.

2 The aluminium attracts the dirt, and the silver comes up bright. Dry thoroughly, and buff to a shine with a soft cloth.

JEWELLERY

The setting and stones of most jewellery need to be cleaned regularly, especially if the piece is worn every day because small particles of dirt can get inside intricate fittings and dislodge the stones. Stones also become dull over time, and settings may tarnish with daily wear.

● Always clean jewellery in a bowl rather than a sink because the stones may work loose and accidentally fall down the plughole.
● Most jewellery can be cleaned in warm, soapy water. Soak the piece in water for a while to loosen the dirt, then brush gently with a soft toothbrush – be careful not to

brush too hard, though, because you may loosen the stones from their settings.
● Use the point of a wooden toothpick to loosen dirt from crevices. I sometimes use toothpaste to clean my rings quickly.
● Cotton buds soaked in a little baking soda solution can also dislodge stubborn dirt.

If you clean special finishes with the wrong cleaners you can ruin them. The following old-fashioned methods help to increase the lifespan of beautiful objects.

GILT
Gold leaf is extremely fragile but does not tarnish easily. Simply wipe carefully with a silk cloth.

LACQUER
Antique lacquer is extremely fragile, easily scratched, and distorted by water. The best way to clean it is to rub it gently with a silk cloth. Modern lacquer can be cleaned with a damp cloth.

MOTHER-OF-PEARL
Clean mother-of-pearl by rubbing with a soft cloth. If it is really dirty, wash it in mild soapy water, but avoid chemical detergents, which may damage the surface.

CHINA & METALWORK

Delicately glazed or hand-painted china, or metalwork such as gilt should always be washed by hand. Washing in the dishwasher will fade, chip, or damage it.

● Rinse china plates immediately after use if they have had acidic food such as tomatoes on them.
● Don't leave delicate china soaking for long because the water may seep under the glaze and damage it.
● Use warm soapy water to clean delicate china. Always wipe clean with a dishcloth rather than a bristle brush.
● Wash china ornaments as above, and use a soft toothbrush to loosen dirt. Wash items one at a time to prevent them knocking against each other and breaking.
● Remove hardwater deposits with vinegar on a damp cloth.

GLASSWARE

Hot, soapy water containing a little vinegar is one of the best ways of cleaning glass. Here are some other tips.

● To clean drinking glasses, squeeze the juice of half a lemon into the water in the washing-up bowl, and add a little washing soda as a water softener. Wash the glasses, then dry immediately to avoid streaking. Polish to a shine with a soft cloth.
● Never apply ammonia to glass because it turns it cloudy.
● Clean glass flower vases each time they are used so that staining does not build up. Soak in neat vinegar or salty water (2 tablespoons salt to 600ml/1 pint water), and rinse thoroughly afterwards.

CRYSTAL

Crystal is more delicate than it looks, and is easily damaged. Follow these tips to help preserve your crystal items.

● Never put crystal into the dishwasher or the microwave: it scratches easily, and goes irreversibly cloudy. Instead, carefully handwash items one at a time in mild soap with a soft brush. Dry immediately.
● To remove wax from a crystal candlestick, allow it to harden first, pull it off, then rub off any residue with ethanol alcohol.

Newly washed crystal should be dried immediately and polished to a sheen with a soft cloth to prevent streaking.

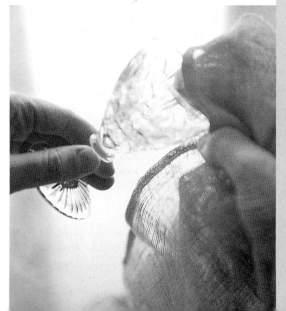

HOUSEHOLD PESTS

Insects and vermin are facts of life and have to be dealt with – but the safe way. Many insecticides are poisonous and should be avoided. Children who are exposed to insecticides are known to have a significantly increased risk of developing a cancer known as non-Hodgkin's lymphoma. There are tried-and-tested natural ways of dealing with household pests that are harmless to humans and leave no damaging traces in the environment. To reduce the incidence of pests, keep your foodstuffs in tightly sealed containers and your storage cupboards clean, don't leave crumbs around, and empty wastebins frequently.

Place muslin sachets of herbs such as dried lavender amongst clothes and bedlinen in drawers to deter moths.

MOTHS

Mothballs contain naphthalene, a highly toxic substance derived from petrochemicals, or the insecticide paradichlorobenzene. Mothball vapours irritate the lungs and can cause kidney and liver damage, headaches, nausea, and depression after prolonged exposure. If you use naphthalene mothballs, reserve them for well-ventilated areas only, separate from your living quarters – or, better still, replace them with natural alternatives.

● Create your own natural moth repellents by filling muslin sachets with dried lavender, a mixture of rosemary and mint, dried tobacco, peppercorns, or cedarwood chips. Place in your drawers among items that are not used frequently. To protect fabric items that are to be stored for a long period, make sure they are completely clean, wrap them in paper, and place in drawers or boxes, with herb sachets.

● If you suspect an infestation, put the items in the freezer for at least 48 hours. Place them in a plastic bag first, squeeze out excess air, then seal tightly. Afterwards, shake them and hang them in the sun. Moth eggs cannot survive extremes of hot and cold.

MICE & RATS

Chemical vermin killers can contain arsenic, strychnine, or phosphorus. Natural alternatives include:
• Keeping a cat to keep mice down, or a terrier for rats.
• Using mousetraps. Keep the bait fresh daily, and place all around the house.

ANTS & COCKROACHES

ANTS
● Sprinkle their trail with baking soda, chilli pepper, paprika, or borax.
● Plant mint just outside your house: ants detest and avoid it.

COCKROACHES
● Make a killer cockroach cocktail. Mix equal parts icing sugar and baking soda or borax. Leave the mixture out near their trail and they won't come back.
● Make a trap by putting chocolate, banana, or raisins in the bottom of a tall glass jar. Smear inside the neck thickly with grease. Cockroaches can climb in but cannot get out.

FLIES

There are several non-toxic ways to repel flies. They dislike citrus scents, so burning lemon or grapefruit oils in a vaporizer will deter them, as will eucalyptus oil. Hang muslin bags filled with cloves around the room, and bunches of eucalyptus, bay, or mint leaves by doors and windows – or spot a few drops of lavender oil inside a lampshade to release its scent when warmed by the heat of the light.

HOMEMADE FLYPAPER

Here is a natural and traditional method of catching flies that gives off no toxic fumes or bad odours. All you need is sugar, golden syrup, and strips of brown parcel wrapping tape.

1 Mix together equal parts by volume of sugar, golden syrup, and water. Boil the mixture until thick, stirring occasionally.

2 Cool, then dip strips of wrapping tape in the sticky mixture. Leave to dry outside for about 30 minutes.

3 Hang up with string. The flies will be attracted to – and trapped on – the sticky coating.

MOSQUITOES

Commercial mosquito repellents contain diethyltoluamide, an irritant that can damage plastic and painted surfaces. Long exposure may, in rare cases, cause tremors and brain disorders, and accidental ingestion has proved fatal to children. Try these natural repellents instead to keep mosquitoes at bay.

- Vinegar repels most insects, including mosquitoes. To use, soak a cotton wool ball in neat vinegar and rub it into your skin daily. This does dry out the skin, however – and may impart a vinegary smell – so you may prefer to combine this remedy with the following scented oil repellent.
- Essential oils of citronella and peppermint both act as powerful deterrents to insects, including mosquitoes. Dilute about 3–4 drops of essential oil in 30ml (1fl oz) base oil, such as sunflower, almond, or wheatgerm. Dab onto your skin in the same way as perfume, once or twice a day.
- Dab neat oils along the hems of your clothes.
- Burn citronella candles, or add a few drops of the essential oil to a vaporizer.
- Mosquitoes are not fast movers, so when they are resting on the wall you can vacuum them up, or use a hand-held bug vacuum, which sucks the insects up into a disposable cartridge.
- Sleep under a mosquito net.

FLEAS & HOUSEMITES
(*See* PEST CONTROL *pages 146–147*)

WASHING & LAUNDRY

Washing requires four simple components: time, motion, water at the right temperature, and chemical action. While the synthetic detergents developed by industrial chemists in the second half of the twentieth century are extremely efficient at cleaning clothes, the "soft chemistry" options have improved with each decade. These vegetable-based cleaning products are derived from natural and renewable sources such as coconut, sugar cane, lemon, spices, chalk, sand, and lime. They do not have harmful side effects, nor do they pollute the environment – and they are often produced in recyclable packaging. Natural soapflakes can also be bought at the supermarket or chemist's for gentle handwashing.

A GENTLER WAY

Apart from using these vegetable-based cleaners, you can minimize your impact on the local and wider ecology by arranging for your power supply to be based on renewable resources (*see Resources page 167*), reducing your energy consumption by making sure that your machine uses hot water from the domestic system, and choosing products that are not tested on animals.

This section is full of energy-saving tips and suggestions for washing clothes and fabrics the natural way, making it safe and healthy both for you and your family – and for the environment, as well.

Hanging just-laundered bedlinen out to dry naturally on a windy day will save energy spent on tumble-drying. It will also give it a delicious fresh-air smell impossible to achieve any other way.

Removing candlewax p68

Keeping colours bright p64

Handwashing delicates p71

De-calcifying a steam iron p73

LAUNDRY KNOW-HOW

Before you wash a new garment or fabric, always make sure that you have read the care label, and organize your washing into separate categories. Restock your utility cupboard with "soft chemistry" washing products and try to eliminate the use of harsh detergents when using a washing machine. Avoid half-loads, as these waste energy, using up a great deal of water and electricity for only a small amount of washing. Fill the drum but do not overload it – leave a "hand-breadth" of space at the top.

Before washing, soak bright-coloured items in a bowl of cold salty water to "fix" the colour so that it will not fade.

ORGANIZING LAUNDRY

To get the best results, separate laundry into different piles according to fabric type – synthetic or natural – and the washing method each type needs – machine-hot, non-colourfast or gentle cycle, or handwashing. This kind of attention will ensure that laundered items last longer.

THE RIGHT CYCLE

- Wash acetates and acrylics, cotton and linen, and wool on different wash cycles.
- Always wash darks separately from lights, and non-fast dyes separately from colourfast items.
- Don't trust delicate items to the machine: wash by hand.

PRE-SOAKING LAUNDRY

- For heavily soiled fabrics, give them a long soak in water before washing. Forget heavy-duty cleaners – water and time are your best allies.
- Treat stains separately (see pages 66–69) before washing.
- To prevent denim from fading, pre-soak items in a solution of vinegar and water (60ml/2fl oz to 5 litres/8 pints water) for 30 minutes.

CUTTING DOWN ON LAUNDRY

- Wear a T-shirt or slip to reduce the need to wash outer garments so often.
- Wear an apron or smock when you are cooking, cleaning, or gardening.
- Avoid lying on the bed in clothes worn outdoors.
- Wash your hands and face before going to bed – a bath or shower is even better – to prevent soiling bedlinen.

HOMEMADE PRE-WASH CLEANER

Follow this recipe to make your own general pre-wash cleaner. It costs next to nothing, and can be made from natural household ingredients. It works well on garments that only need a quick spot-clean before washing, or that are dry-clean-only. Keep it for occasional use. It will keep indefinitely if stored in a cool, dry place.

YOU WILL NEED:
115ml (4fl oz) white vinegar
2 tablespoons ammonia
4 tablespoons baking soda
2 tablespoons liquid soap

1 Place all the ingredients together in a glass bowl and stir until thoroughly mixed. Pour into a screw-top jar.

2 Shake the mixture vigorously before use. Dab it on with a clean cloth, and rinse off after 1 minute.

SOFT & SWEET

Fabric conditioners help sustain the suppleness of fibres and reduce static. Instead, try "soft chemistry" products based on natural fatty acids from vegetable sources, such as coconut oil or lecithin (*see Resources page 167*) – or make your own.

● If you live in a hard-water area, try adding 1 tablespoon of white vinegar to the fabric conditioner compartment of the washing machine. In my experience, this has just the same effect as a manufactured chemical conditioner.

● Many synthetic fragrances added to laundry products contain allergenic chemicals. To make your washing smell good, mix the vinegar conditioner (*right*) with 4–5 drops of essential oil – lemon or lavender are favourites.

HOMEMADE FABRIC CONDITIONER

Mix together 1 cup each of washing soda, white vinegar, and water. Stir in a few drops of essential oil (lavender, lemon, cedarwood, or geranium). Store in a screw-top bottle, and use as you would a commercial conditioner.

TIPS FOR MACHINE-WASHING

However gentle the setting, the mechanical action of the washing cycle as items of clothing are turned in the drum is fairly vigorous. To keep clothing in good condition over a lifetime of machine-washing, follow these guidelines.

● Check all pockets are empty.
● Turn corduroy inside out, or else the pile will pick up fluff and fibres from other fabrics.
● Turn denim jeans inside out to prevent them from fading.
● Machine-washable knitwear

may "pill", and benefits from being turned inside out.
● Rub a moistened bar of mild soap over dirt lines on shirt collars and cuffs, then brush with an old toothbrush to loosen dirt before washing.

● Place delicate fabrics inside a pillowcase to protect them inside the machine drum.
● Soak soiled handkerchiefs overnight in salty water (1 tablespoon to 600ml/1 pint) before machine washing.

NATURAL STAIN REMOVERS

There are several "soft chemistry" stain removers to turn to in an emergency. These contain solvents based on ethanol (the same alcohol that is present in wine and beer), which breaks down rapidly in the environment and has no known side effects. Glycerine, a by-product of soap manufacture, is an effective cleaning agent that is available from most chemists. Washing soda is one of the oldest products used for cleaning. It is also a natural water softener and helps remove grease as well as dirt. Turpentine is a mild, natural solvent for oily stains. As well as being effective on fabric, it can be used to clean brushes used with oil-based paints, and its method of production encourages sustainable forestry practices.

PRODUCTS TO AVOID

The following substances are all strong chemical stain removers: they emit vapour, cause damage to eyes and skin on contact, and may be based on unsustainable resources. Chemical solvents may also leave marks at the edge of treated stains, which are then difficult to remove.

SAFETY FIRST

Keep all cleaning materials out of reach of children.

•

Always read the instructions.

•

When using chemicals, wear rubber gloves and goggles.

•

Never mix chemical cleaners together since they give off toxic fumes.

•

Stop using the product if you feel dizzy, nauseous, or develop a headache.

COMMERCIAL STAIN OR SPOT REMOVERS

Some of these may contain, amongst other ingredients, dry-cleaning solvents such as perchloroethylene (*see page 73*) and trichloroethylene, petroleum-based compounds. Sodium hypochlorite, an essential component of bleach (*see below*), may also be an ingredient in some removers.

ACETONE

The main ingredient in nail polish removers, with a distinctive sweet odour, acetone may remove certain stains but it is so powerful that it melts man-made cellulose fibres and removes dye colour from other synthetic fibres. It is irritating to the eyes, nose, and throat.

CHLORINE BLEACH

Bleach damages natural fibres – your beautiful wools and silks and jerseys and velvets will be ruined. It is irritating to skin, eyes, and the respiratory tract.

METHYLATED SPIRIT AND WHITE SPIRIT

Both are derived from petrochemicals and are neither sustainable nor ecologically sound. Avoid them completely.

METHANOL

A type of alcohol, this is a wood derivative, also known as wood alcohol, wood spirits, or methyl alcohol. It was once used by hat-makers to dilute their colours and mould their forms. The fumes not only caused blindness but sent them mad, hence the saying "as mad as a hatter". Sometimes present in paint removers, it is a severe skin and eye irritant.

ISOPROPYL ALCOHOL

Used to treat a range of stains. This is a petrochemical derivative, and is to be avoided.

THE WATER TREATMENT

Nature's greatest solvent is water, and this, coupled with speedy action on your part, is the key to successful stain removal. When an accident occurs, do the following:

- Mop up any excess at once with absorbent kitchen towel.
- Soak the stained area with lukewarm water (not hot – this may "cook" the stain and set it). Soda water and sparkling water are both excellent solvents, especially for treating red wine spills (*see also page 67*) and removing pet stains.
- Never rub hard – just dab, so as not to damage fibres.
- Work the stain from the inside outwards.

REMOVING PROTEIN STAINS

To remove stains such as blood and egg (but not butter, which is a grease stain), try the following. Do not use hot water (this "fixes" the stain), but soak in lukewarm water and apply a soap-based or salt solution before washing.

- Egg stains on clothes and soft furnishings respond well to a solution of borax (*see below*), or to soaking in salt water. Scrape off as much egg as you can first with a dull blade before treating the fabric.
- The albumen protein in bloodstains is broken down by salt, so soak in cold salty water while the stain is fresh.
- Chocolate stains can be easily removed with lukewarm soapy water or borax solution (*see below*), or try using glycerine. Soak the stained fabric in a bowl of glycerine for 30 minutes, then rinse out.
- For a dried-on protein stain, dab with a little ammonia diluted with cold water.

STAIN REMOVER CHECKLIST

Washing soda (sodium carbonate)
White vinegar
Fresh lemon
Salt (sodium chloride)
Baking soda (sodium bicarbonate)
Turpentine
Glycerine
Fuller's earth (for grease stains)

For occasional use in small amounts only:
Ethanol (pure alcohol)
Borax
Ammonia

HOMEMADE BORAX STAIN REMOVER

This stain remover works well on protein stains. Have a supply ready-mixed for emergency stain removal.

YOU WILL NEED:
25g (1oz) borax
600ml (1 pint) cold water

1 Fill a screw-top bottle with the correct quantity of water, and add the borax.

2 Replace the top of the bottle and shake the solution well, to mix.

3 Dab the solution onto the stain with a clean cloth. Leave to dry, then launder.

REMOVING COLOURED STAINS

The following tips suggest ways to remove coloured food and drink stains. Berry fruits, coffee, tea, and red wine are among the most tiresome but, if you act quickly, they can be removed without recourse to chemicals.

● Apply a dab of fresh lemon juice or white vinegar to the stain, or soak the stain in a "soft chemistry" bleach before laundering.

● For wine stains on clothes, pour salt onto the affected area to absorb the moisture before soaking the garment in a "soft chemistry" bleach. Or splash with soda water, then launder.

● For old red wine stains, try using the glycerine method given for chocolate stains (see page 67). This stain-removal technique also works for beetroot, red cabbage, and dark fruit stains.

● When red wine is spilt on carpet, mop up the excess liquid and then pour white wine over the patch to saturate it. Let the wine soak into the carpet fibres for 10 minutes, then rinse with lukewarm water.

● To remove tea or coffee stains, work glycerine into the area. Leave the glycerine to soak into the fabric, and then rinse out with warm water.

● For tea-stained upholstery, use homemade borax stain remover (see page 67). Treat coffee stains in the same way.

● Soak grass stains in glycerine before laundering. This works well on cricket and tennis whites, which are prone to grass staining. Soak in a solution of washing soda (110g/4oz to 5 litres/1 gallon water), then rinse.

Dabbing a soft fruit juice stain with freshly squeezed lemon juice will bleach out the colour naturally.

REMOVING GREASE STAINS

The following tips work on greasy make-up stains, candle-wax spills, butter, margarine, mayonnaise, cooking oils, and engine oil.

● Pre-treat the oiled fabric with baking soda paste (see page 52), then soak in warm water with a "soft chemistry" washing powder. For the machine-wash, add 2 tablespoons of baking soda to your washing powder.

● Dab neat ethanol alcohol on obstinate stains.

● Draw out ordinary grease stains by covering with a generous sprinkling of fuller's earth powder. Leave it on for several hours or overnight, then brush off with a stiff bristle brush. This also works well on cooking fat.

● Dab lipstick stains with eucalyptus oil. Leave

To remove wax, place brown paper over the wax stain and melt it with a warm iron. It will lift off onto the paper.

the oil to soak in before laundering the garment. Lipstick and cosmetic stains can also be treated as for grass stains (*see opposite*).

● White handkerchiefs and table napkins stained with lipstick can be boiled clean in hot water.

● Treat oil, tar, and grass stains with a few drops of eucalyptus oil. Rub the essential oil into the stain, then launder the fabric as usual.

● Rub lard into tar stains, then wash the article, adding 2 tablespoons of washing soda to your washing powder.

COMMON HOUSEHOLD STAINS

Most sticky household stains and coloured marks can be removed using natural ingredients and the bleaching effect of sunlight. You should rarely need to use chemical bleach or any of the proprietary stain removers on the market.

● For sticky substances such as glue or chewing gum, first scratch off as much of the substance as possible, then use a citrus cleaner (*see Resources page 167*).

● Chewing gum on clothes may also be treated by holding the affected item over a steaming kettle until the gum is soft enough to pull off, taking particular care not to damage fabric that has a pile. Alternatively, place the garment in the freezer compartment. When the chewing gum is frozen, it can be lifted.

● Remove washing powder residues (left on fabric when washed in an over-full machine) by giving the item a second rinse.

● Scrape off shoe polish, then dab the affected area with neat ethanol alcohol.

● Soak rust stains for 20–30 minutes in a solution made from the juice of 1 lemon mixed with 1 heaped tablespoon of table salt. Rub well, then wash and dry outside in the sun to bleach. Repeat the process until the stain has disappeared.

● Soak sweat stains in water to which 1–2 tablespoons of white vinegar or lemon juice, or a handful of baking soda, has been added. Wash the article according to the care instructions on the label.

SCORCH MARKS

Remove scorch marks with the simplest of remedies – lemon juice and sunlight.

When ironing fabrics on too hot a setting, you may scorch the material. If the scorching is light, and the affected item is 100 per cent cotton, such as a napkin, the lemon juice method works well. First soak the scorched area in pure, freshly squeezed lemon juice. Rinse out in warm water and then leave outside to dry in sunlight and benefit from the bleaching action of the sun. Alternatively, use a "soft chemistry" bleach.

Apply lemon juice to the scorched area and place in the sun. Then machine-wash with a "soft chemistry" powder.

WASHING THE NATURAL WAY

Doing your laundry the natural way has a number of benefits. "Soft chemistry" or homemade powders and liquids are less harsh on the fibres of the fabric, and also limit the quantity of chemicals entering rivers and lakes. They are kinder on the skin, and seem to cause fewer allergic reactions. In contrast, commercial laundry products are based on petrochemicals and contain phosphates, enzymes, and bleaches that are highly toxic. When chemical detergents (described as "surfactants" on labels) soak away from your drains, they can damage fish, animal, and plant life. Before buying any product, check to see what it really contains.

HOMEMADE POWDER

To make your own allergy-free washing powder, mix together 50g (2oz) of soapflakes with 25g (1oz) washing soda. Add a bit more washing soda to the mix if you live in a hard-water area.

CHOOSING PRODUCTS

"Soft chemistry" products, based on soaps made from coconut, palm, and rapeseed oils, are the best option for laundry (*see Resources page 167*). Of the more conventional alternatives, washing powder, ideally in concentrated form, is preferable to liquid products, which contain three to four times more petrochemical-based detergent. Try using half the recommended amount: your wash should come out just as clean, while reducing the tendency for a build up of soap residues in fibres.

● Check the ingredients listed to make sure that the product is based on vegetable and mineral sources. Check that it is biodegradable, and has not been tested on animals.

● "Biological" washing powders contain enzymes that are added to products to help remove protein stains. The enzymes are active only at low temperatures, thus reducing energy costs. However, enzymes can affect other protein molecules too, including human ones, and are thought to increase the incidence of allergic reactions.

Check that your washing powder is enzyme-free, and use natural stain removers (*see pages 66–69*).
● Optical brighteners, designed to make your washing come out "whiter than white", are derived from petrochemicals, and do not biodegrade easily. They also cause skin allergies and hinder wound healing.

Laundry balls are eco-friendly, using only the cleansing power of water.

LAUNDRY BALLS

This new "green" washing product claims to replace the need for powder or liquid laundry detergents. It works by producing ionized oxygen that activates water molecules, making them penetrate deeply into fibres to shift dirt.

● The balls are hypoallergenic and suitable for sensitive skin.
● They save water – a second rinse is unnecessary.
● They can be re-used up to 750 times, making them excellent value (*see Resources page 167*).

CHEMICAL & NATURAL BLEACHES

Use natural or "soft chemistry" alternatives to chlorine bleach wherever possible.

● Chlorine bleach can be hazardous (see page 66), and it pollutes the water supply. Chlorine products should not be mixed with ammonia or acid-based cleaners (including vinegar): the compound produced gives off chloramine, which causes lung problems.

● Powdered bleaches containing borax are active over 60°C (140°F). Boron, a constituent of borax, is a harmful chemical.

● Bleach made from percarbonate is the most environmentally sound chemical bleach. Percarbonate contains soda and oxygenated water so it is entirely natural (see Resources page 167).

● To revive whites, boil them in water with a little soap powder and fresh lemon. Simmer for 10 minutes. The lemon acts as a bleaching agent. (Never boil synthetics.)

USING YOUR MACHINE

If you live in a hard-water area, calcium deposits will build up in parts of your washing machine. These threaten its efficiency and shorten its working life. Here's what to do:

● Add 1-2 tablespoons of washing soda to the detergent drawer of your washing machine to reduce calcium deposits. This also reduces the amount of commercial powder you need by up to 30 per cent.

Add washing soda to reduce the amount of detergent you have to use.

● Use powders or washing liquids that contain ecological water-softening agents such as zeolite or citrate. EDTA and NTA, which are widely used in commercial washing powders, are made from petrochemicals, do not biodegrade readily, and are a particular hazard to drinking water.

HANDWASHING

If the label states that a fabric should be handwashed, do not risk machine-washing. Handwash the item in natural soapflakes, or a "soft chemistry" liquid wool-wash based on coconut oil (see Resources page 167).

● Pre-soak the fabric in water with mild soapflakes to loosen dirt and grime.
● Rinse out soapflakes in lukewarm water until the fabric no longer feels slippery to the touch.
● For extra body and softness, add 1 tablespoon of baking soda to the last rinse.
● If washing silk, add a dash of vinegar to the final rinse to improve the shine.
● Dry flat on a clean towel in a warm place.

After rinsing, wrap delicate handwashed garments in a towel and press out any excess moisture.

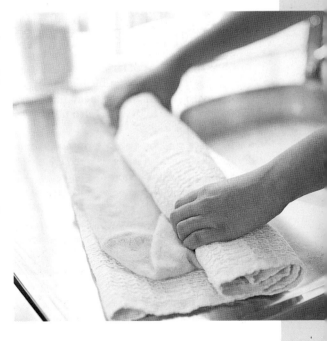

RECYCLING WASTE

It may come as a surprise but more than two-thirds of the materials we throw away as rubbish can be recycled. By changing our habits, the three key practices – reduce, reuse, and recycle – will become second nature. The secret is to make it easy for yourself and to organize good recycling facilities in your home so that the process becomes routine.

THE BENEFITS OF RECYCLING

Recycling is really just a matter of reusing items instead of throwing them away. It increases awareness of the amount of waste we produce and gives us a greater sense of collective responsibility as consumers. Old glass bottles go to manufacture new bottles and other glassware, paper is recycled into stationery and newsprint, and plastic is melted down to make containers, garden furniture, and even clothes. Aluminium and steel are recycled into new cans, and organic waste creates rich nutrients when composted for your garden.

RECYCLING FACILITIES

Find out about local recycling facilities. Some local authorities have recycling centres where a range of waste materials can be taken for processing – some even offer kerbside collection. If you do not have home collection, take your recyclable waste with you on your weekly supermarket shopping trips, since most superstores provide recycling containers for paper, glass, and metal. Allow reusing and recycling to become part of your thinking and part of your life.

Many household items can be recycled. All you need is a little organization and practical storage facilities.

Storing recyclable items p79

Reusing wooden boxes p81

Collecting organic waste p82

Recycling waste paper p86

HEALTHY FOOD

Eating well, and enjoying fresh healthy food in all its variety, is life-enhancing. In the developed world, we are faced with more choices about how and what we eat than ever before. More and more people are choosing to eat organically grown food, believing that it is more nutritious and less contaminated than mainstream food products. There is indeed evidence to suggest that organic foods contain fewer traces of pesticides and fertilizers, and that vegetables and fruits ripened in the sun – instead of grown on a large scale under glass – contain more nutrients. Personally, I prefer to eat organic food because I think it tastes better. For those concerned about animal rights, it is reassuring to know that animal welfare is an important part of the organic farming ethos. Although organic items are a little more expensive, often the food goes further because it has a lower water content and higher nutritional value.

DEVELOPING AWARENESS

The more awareness we bring to the activity of preparing and eating food, the healthier, safer, and more harmonious our lives will become. How our food is grown, transported, and packaged all have an impact on the environment. Choosing fair trade products helps to ensure basic rights for food producers in less developed countries. Buying fresh food locally is not only healthier but kinder to the environment. Gardeners can play their part, too, in halting the disappearance of traditional fruit and vegetable varieties by growing their own.

An organic vegetable box can be delivered to your door in some areas. Many farms offer this service direct.

Fruit and vegetable juices p90

Key foods to buy organic p94

Natural food additives p96

Kitchen hygiene p106

A GOOD DIET

Although there is much advice about what constitutes a healthy diet, the consensus based on health studies is that we thrive when our diet consists of about 60 per cent complex carbohydrates, 25 per cent fats, and 15 per cent proteins. A good diet is a varied diet, and eating plenty of fresh vegetables – both cooked and raw – and fresh and dried fruit provides us with many of the nutrients, vitamins, and minerals that we need. Whole grains and pulses provide the remainder of the complex carbohydrates. Our protein comes from smaller amounts of lean meat, poultry, and fish, some dairy produce, and seeds and nuts.

Drinking freshly pressed fruit or vegetable juice is another way to increase your fruit and vegetable intake.

"FIVE SERVINGS A DAY"

Current nutritional advice is to eat a minimum of "five servings" of fruit and vegetables daily. It sounds like a lot until you understand that a "serving" in these terms is only the size of a fistful of food. One of the best ways of ensuring that you do so is to eat fresh fruit or vegetables as snacks. Eat these foods as fresh as possible: the longer that fruit and vegetables are stored, the greater the loss of nutrients. The following are some useful examples of the equivalent of one serving:

- 1 medium-sized apple
- 1 large carrot
- 1 banana
- 100g (4oz) cooked or raw vegetables, salad or fruit
- 1 small handful of dried fruit (around 50g/2oz)

SUGAR & FATS

The accepted wisdom among nutritionists is to eat a low-sugar, low-fat diet. Refined sugars are an unnecessary part of our diet: small amounts are fine, but to rely on them for energy leads to malnourishment and obesity. The body manufactures its own sugars from the complex carbohydrates that we eat, and will maintain stamina far better than with a "sugar rush" induced by eating chocolate, cake, or biscuits. Try to ration your intake of foods that contain refined sugars and fats to the occasional treat.

A small portion of fresh vegetable soup is equivalent to one serving but this generous bowl of soup probably equals three.

ARTIFICIAL SWEETENERS

These are best avoided since the effects of aspartame, acesulfame, and sucralose are not fully known. Use natural sweeteners such as cane juice, fruit juice, or honey instead.

FATTY ACIDS

The right amounts of the right fats are essential for good health. Certain fatty acids are essential for nourishing body tissue (which includes the brain). Linoleic acid (LA), or omega-6, and alpha-linoleic acid (ALA), or omega-3, are especially important for health. Corn, sesame seed, sunflower, safflower, and wheatgerm oils contain LA, and oils derived from flaxseed, walnut, hemp seed, soya bean, and rapeseed all contain ALA. Seed oils should be unrefined and preferably "cold-pressed" or "virgin" since heat and light can destroy the essential fatty acids they contain. Fish such as salmon, mackerel, and herring contain ALA derivatives that have many positive health benefits, so regular amounts of these fish are important in a balanced diet.

PROBIOTICS

Probiotics are bacteria that keep the intestinal tract healthy. They are found in miso (fermented soya) and yogurt, so include these in your diet.

FATS TO AVOID

The following fats are best left out of your diet, or only used occasionally: saturated and trans-fats found in fatty meat and processed foods; refined vegetable oils; hydrogenated oils such as in margarine; and fats used in fried foods.

MEAL PLANNING

As well as having a varied diet, many people find huge health benefits from ensuring that their meals are balanced correctly, in line with the "food combining" system devised by Dr. William Howard Hay in the early twentieth century. Because proteins and starches are digested differently by the body, Dr. Hay's diet separates these and other foods into compatible and non-compatible groups.

The principles of this diet are to plan your meals so that they are protein-based or starch-based, with neutral foods that can be eaten with either of these two. Starch and sugar should not be eaten with proteins, and fruit is best eaten separately. Root vegetables, such as beetroot, potatoes, and Jerusalem artichokes, are fine with a carbohydrate meal but not with protein meal, due to their high carbohydrate content. For example, eat fish without the chips or bread, but with lots of vegetables and salad instead.

GUIDELINES FOR FOOD COMBINING

● Allow salads, vegetables, and fruit to form the major part of your diet.
● Eat proteins, starches, and fats in small quantities, and never eat them together at the same meal.
● Avoid processed foods, particularly white flour and sugar. Use only wholegrains and unprocessed starches.
● Always leave about four hours between meals so that the digestive process can be completed.
● Refined sugars are not useful, so avoid desserts and sweets.
● All green vegetables and salads are neutral foods, and can be combined with protein or carbohydrates.
● Eat melons and citrus fruits on their own.

A small piece of grilled fish served with a large selection of steamed vegetables is good food combining.

Certain fruits and vegetables are best bought or grown organically as they may harbour higher levels of toxic residues than other foods.

FOODS VULNERABLE TO RESIDUES

If you are concerned about the safety levels of some of the food you eat, there are certain fruits and vegetables that retain more chemical residues than others. While stating that "legal limits do not define safety", a 1999 analysis of US government data on pesticide residues in foods supplied a toxicity index of pesticide contamination, giving a breakdown of the levels, listed below. Check this list to see which foods it is best to buy organic.

TOXICITY INDEX

HIGH	MEDIUM	LOWER
Peaches	Apples	Apricots
Squash	Bananas	Chocolate
	Grapes	Eggs
	Green beans	Fish
	Milk	Grains
	Peas	Lettuce
	Spinach	Oranges
	Strawberries	Meat

ORGANIC CERTIFICATION

Certified organic growers have to follow strict guidelines for food production. For example, they are not allowed to use sewage sludge to enrich the soil, whereas commercial growers are permitted to do so. By law, foods can only be sold as "organic" if they have been certified by official, regulatory bodies, which vary from country to country (*see Resources page 169*).

ORGANIC MEAT & FISH

Eating organic meat and fish whenever possible means that you will be furthering animal rights and also, by buying lesser-known breeds, supporting biodiversity.

WHY CHOOSE ORGANIC?

Eating meat raises a number of environmental and ethical issues, some of which can be avoided by choosing organic.
● Intensively reared animals are often kept in dark, crowded conditions, and are fed drugs such as growth-stimulating hormones, steroids, sulfadrugs, colourings and flavourings.
● Milk from dairy cattle, and cheese made from it, may contain DDT residues, antibiotics, hormones such as

REMOVING RESIDUES

When eating non-organic fruits and vegetables, it is recommended that you wash them thoroughly to remove as many chemical residues as possible, and that you peel fruit and root vegetables – experts recommend always peeling the skins of peaches, apples, pears, and grapes. Washing fruit and vegetables with washing-up liquid is said to be very effective in removing surface residues, but make sure this is a "soft chemistry" variety and give the items a good rinse in water afterwards.

bovine growth hormone, and mastitis bacteria. It may also be homogenized, which can lead to heart disease in humans.

● More than half the world's antibiotics are used to promote growth in animals reared for meat.

● A high proportion of poultry and meat products produced from intensively farmed meat may be infected with salmonella, campylobacter, or *E. coli*.

● Unlike intensively reared animals, organic livestock spend much of their time outdoors, grazing on organic pastures. The animals are raised in closed, self-regenerating herds, and many are kept in family groups.

● Organic animals are not given unnecessary medication, and wherever possible are treated with natural remedies. Animals are allowed to mature naturally, without the aid of growth-promoting agents .

● If you eat a lot of meat, try to cut down on the amount. Two thirds of the worlds' agricultural land is used for raising livestock, which could otherwise be under crop cultivation with far higher food yields.

Eggs, fish, milk, grains, and chocolate may store medium to low levels of toxins, and if possible are best bought organic for ethical as well as health reasons.

EATING FRESH FISH

Farmed fish – usually salmon and trout – are kept in restricted tanks, in water cleaned with chemicals. They are fed on a diet of rich processed foods to build up their body fat. Living in confined quarters, they are prone to lice, for which they are treated with antibiotics. Buy organic fish when you shop and eat out.

● Wild fish, if caught in coastal waters, may be contaminated with industrial pollution. Shellfish, in particular, can be highly polluted because they live in coastal habitats.

● Larger fish contain more contaminants and should be avoided, especially by pregnant women, because they may contain high levels of methylmercury, which can harm an unborn child's nervous system. Swordfish, marlin, shark, king mackerel, and tilefish are the worst offenders.

● Largely herbivorous fish such as tilapia, catfish, red and sockeye salmon, and wild trout are less likely to be contaminated, as are deep-water fish such as sardines.

● When cleaning the fish, remove as much surface fat as possible, as this is where the bulk of the chemical contaminants are stored.

● The way the fish is cooked can help to reduce the traces of chemicals in the body fat, skin, and muscle tissue: grilling, baking, and steaming allow the juices and fats to run off, whereas frying and making soups reserve the fat.

READING THE LABEL

Foods contain additives for several reasons: to replace the nutritional value lost in processing; to enhance their texture or appearance; and to offer a longer shelf-life, or to facilitate the preparation of the processed food. It is not always possible to tell from reading the food product label whether the additives come from natural or chemical sources, as this is not a legal requirement. The best advice I can offer to the consumer is to choose a product labelled as "natural", although labelling is not necessarily 100 per cent accurate .

FOOD ADDITIVES

Producers do not have to declare whether pesticides have been used in the cultivation of fresh fruit and vegetables, and the law does not require many additives in processed foods to be labelled as such. The fact that substances are "approved" by food standards authorities does not always mean that they are safe, since the long-term effects may not have been fully tested.

IRRADIATION

Some foods are irradiated with a dose of radiation about 60 million times that of a chest X-ray. This is to kill insects and bacteria, and to prevent sprouting and slow rotting. It destroys at least 10 per cent of the vitamin content, and alters the chemical structure of the food. No long-term safety studies have been carried out, although irradiation is suspected of causing leukaemia and other cancers in humans, and kidney disease. In many countries, irradiated food must be labelled as such: look for the logo, and, where possible, try to avoid all irradiated foodstuffs.

NATURAL ADDITIVES

The following additives come from natural plant and animal sources and are a safe alternative to chemical additives and colourings. Look for them in the ingredients list on the label.

- Acetic acid (vinegar)
- Sodium chloride (salt)
- Albumen (from egg white)
- Annatto (an extract from a rainforest tree)
- Beta-carotene (from carrots)
- Citric acid (from citrus fruits)
- Dextrose (from corn sugar)
- Guar gum (from a seed grown in India)
- Gum tragacanth (from a thorny shrub native to the Middle East)
- Lactic acid (from whey, cornstarch, potatoes, and molasses)
- Lecithin (a substance occurring naturally in eggs, soya beans, and corn)

Agar-agar, carragheen, dulse, and alginates from seaweed contain valuable minerals and flavour food naturally.

ADDITIVES TO AVOID

Read packaging carefully and try to avoid the following.

SULPHITES

These additives are used in foods to prevent spoiling and discolouration, and are listed as sulphur dioxide, sodium sulphite, sodium and potassium bisulphite or metabisulphite. They can trigger severe allergic reactions, including nausea and vomiting, breathing difficulties, and abdominal pain. Asthmatics are especially susceptible. Sulphites are found in wine, shellfish, fruit and vegetables, salad dressings, sauces, and corn syrup. They may be used in self-service salad bars to keep food looking fresh. In the US, foods to be eaten raw may not be treated with sulphites.

NITRATES & NITRITES

These additives are used to enhance colour and inhibit the growth of the botulism bacteria in cured meats (especially pork), fish and cheese, sausages, luncheon meats, and hot dogs. A percentage of nitrates convert to nitrites once ingested, which may then combine with amines (proteins in food) to form carcinogenic nitrosamines.

However, there is as yet no compelling evidence that eating nitrates or nitrites poses a risk to humans.

ARTIFICIAL COLOURS & FLAVOURINGS

Almost all artificial colourings have been shown to be carcinogenic in animals. The observations of doctors and parents have been that when artificial colourings and flavourings are avoided, children's hyperactivity and other behavioural problems improve significantly.

MSG

Monosodium glutamate is a flavour enhancer often used in Chinese restaurant food. It can cause headaches, cold sweats, and heart palpitations. Studies show that MSG can cause brain damage and female sterility in animals.

EDTA

Ethylenediaminetetraacetic acid is used as a preservative in processed foods, and may have toxic effects. Symptoms recorded by those with high exposure to it include dizziness, headaches, sneezing, nausea, and asthma attacks.

Salt and sugar are natural additives. Use them in moderation and avoid processed foods, which contain high quantities of both.

E-NUMBERS

There is a complete list of e-numbers – European Union permitted additives – available on the internet (see Resources page 169). The ones listed here have been linked to health problems, including asthma.

E 100–180 (colouring agents)
E 102 (the yellow colouring

tartrazine, which is linked to allergies and adverse reactions)
E 200–290 (preservatives)
E 300–322 (antioxidants)
E 400–495 (emulsifiers and stabilizers)
E 420–421 (sweeteners)
E 173 (aluminium, which has been linked to senile dementia and Alzheimer's disease)

GENETICALLY MODIFIED (GM) FOODS

Genetically engineering food means manipulating DNA to increase yield and strengthen resistance to disease. In plants this helps to control pests and weeds and to enhance nutritional value. However, many people are concerned about the impact GM crops could have on wildlife because they disturb the natural ecological balance, and about the transfer of genetic modifications to wild plant species. The long-term effects on humans of eating GM foods is not yet known. If you want to avoid them, look for "GM-free" or "no GMOs" labels on foods.

WHAT WE DRINK

Water is vital to good health: after all, the human body is made up of over 70 per cent water. Although the water that comes out of your tap is treated to make it as safe as possible to drink (*see page 15*), unfortunately these measures by no means remove all contaminants. In some countries (the United States, Australia, New Zealand, and parts of Europe), the water is also fluoridated to prevent tooth decay, but there are concerns about the long-term health effects of fluoridation.

CONTAMINANTS IN THE WATER SUPPLY

According to the Worldwatch Institute in the US, it is more important now than ever before to protect the water supply from chemical abuse. Groundwater pollution is effectively permanent. It is not uncommon for the contaminants listed below to be found in public water supplies. Between them, these contaminants have been found to cause birth defects; reproductive system damage; cancer; liver, kidney and nervous system damage; and gastroenteric diseases. But it isn't all bad news – over 95 per cent of these chemicals can be removed by using water filters.

WATER DISINFECTANTS
The most widely used is chlorine, but chloramine and chlorine dioxide, weaker forms of chlorine, may also be used. They are all known irritants. Of particular concern is the reaction of chlorine with organic matter in the water to produce disinfectant by-products such as trihalomethanes (including chloroform), dangerous compounds that have been linked to cancer.

VOLATILE ORGANIC COMPOUNDS (VOCS)
These derive mainly from industrial chemicals and solvents (e.g. benzene, toluene, vinyl chloride), and also from household cleaning products.

TRACE METALS
These include heavy metals such as lead, mercury, arsenic, aluminium, cadmium, copper, chromium, and the radiological contaminant radon.

SYNTHETIC ORGANIC CHEMICALS
Drinking water may contain many synthetic organic chemicals (*see page 93*). High levels of nitrates from fertilizers are a concern as they are linked to a number of health risks.

MICROBES
Two harmful microbes found in drinking water are the parasites *Cryptosporidium* and *Giardia*; both cause gastric illness.

HOW SAFE IS BOTTLED WATER?

European standards for factory bottled water are lower than for tap water. Federal rules in the US specify no protection of bottled water sources, although they do so for tap water.

● Disinfection to eliminate contaminants is common practice, adding extra chemicals such as chlorine, which can create by-products.
● Bottled water may not be fresh: in many countries there is no legal requirement to put a sell-by date on the label.
● Many manufacturers use plastic bottles that leach polymers into the water, are not degradable, and sit in landfill sites.
● Fluoride levels can be five times higher than in tap water.

FILTER YOUR WATER

Health experts recommend drinking 1–2 litres (1¾–3½ pints) of water per day. Water company data will tell you the quality of our water as it leaves the treatment plant but not as it comes out of your tap, so it makes sense to filter it.

ASSESSING WATER QUALITY

Find out the answers to these questions to help you decide what kind of water purification system you need (*see below*).
● Where does your water come from?
● Are you near industrial sites that emit toxic waste, or agricultural land that uses pesticides and fertilizers?
● Is your water carried into your home by lead piping?
● Is chlorine used to disinfect it? Is it fluoridated?

Herbal infusions use boiling water and are a purer way of drinking tap water.

CARBON FILTRATION
All activated carbon filtration systems – water-jug filters, counter-top and under-sink filters – will remove chlorine and its by-products, organic chemicals, and VOCs, and improve the taste of your water. They may include an ion-exchange resin that will sift out heavy metals such as lead and aluminium. They will not remove fluoride, nitrates, or microbes. However, systems with solid carbon block filters (often the plumbed-in variety) that have a very small pore size will filter out certain microbes.

REVERSE OSMOSIS
The most effective systems filter water through activated carbon and then a semi-permeable membrane that rejects minerals, trace metals, fluoride, nitrates, microbes, and a range of other impurities, while improving flavour.

COFFEE & TEA

Tea and coffee are both popular alternatives to drinking a glass of water. But remember, both contain caffeine and are mildly diuretic.

Use unbleached coffee filter papers for preference, or opt for white, oxygen-cleansed ones.

● Tea plantations use many pesticides, some of them very toxic and banned in the West.
● Many tea bags are bleached using chlorine, and may leach dioxins into your tea. Use loose leaf teas and a teapot instead.
● Green tea is healthier than black tea because it is not fermented, and so contains numerous vitamins and minerals. Medical research shows that green tea prevents tooth decay, reduces halitosis, and boosts the immune system against flu, some cancers, and heart disease.

● Many coffee plantations use pesticides that are banned in the US and Europe. These pollute local water supplies and damage the health of the plantation workers.
● Instant coffee may contain artificial flavours.
● Decaffeinated coffee may be processed with the solvents hexane, a component of which is known to cause nerve damage, and methylene chloride, which is also found in paint remover and is a probable human carcinogen. Choose water-processed brands.

FOOD SUPPLIERS

Buying for food has become increasingly centred on the supermarket as it is an easy and convenient way to shop. Because most people prefer to shop for a week's food supply in one trip, and many stores are located away from the high street, supermarket shopping is geared around the car – an unecological factor in more ways than simply using petrol. One of the attractions of the supermarket is the huge choice on the shelves. However, many of the goods will have been transported from all over the world, and, to arrive "fresh", will have used up electricity for refrigeration, preservatives, and aviation fuel. Supermarkets factor in a staggering waste margin: huge quantities of perishable foods are disposed of once their "shelf-life" is over. However, some supermarket chains now compost fruit and vegetables past their prime.

HOW TO SHOP ECOLOGICALLY

Use the supermarket when you need to, but also consider some of the alternatives listed here. Smaller food outlets will tend to specialize, offering quality over quantity.

Aim to buy locally produced foods in season when they are plentiful, offer the best quality , and are inexpensive.

SHOP LOCALLY

If possible, walk or cycle to the shops rather than taking the car, and use local markets and high streets. This may well save time by avoiding traffic jams and long supermarket check-out queues. It also saves petrol and transport costs, keeps local people in business, and supports the community. This kind of shopping is more personal. Shopping little and often means less waste and fresher food.

BUY LOCAL PRODUCE

Farmers' markets are taking an increasing share of the food business, and local producers still make cheeses or sell cream from the local dairy. There are no middlemen involved, so their prices are often lower.

PROMOTE BIODIVERSITY

Choose old-fashioned or unusual varieties of fruits and vegetables, and buy meat from farmers who raise rare breed livestock.

ORGANIC BOX DELIVERY

There are many local organic home delivery services now available. You simply phone, fax, or email through your order to the supplier, and it arrives on your doorstep at the arranged hour. This saves you time and fuel, and it is much more economical for one van to deliver to many addresses. Your local supermarket may even have such a scheme. If you do join a supermarket delivery service, ask for organic and GM-free products – businesses respond to consumer demand.

FAIR TRADE GOODS

Whenever possible, buy food produce displaying the Fair Trade label (*see Resources page 169*). A number of products, such as coffee, tea, chocolate, bananas, sugar, honey, biscuits, drinking cocoa, orange juice, muesli, rice, and dried fruits, are all available, and the range is expanding all the time.

ORGANIC SUPERMARKETS

Increasingly, there are a number of specialist organic supermarkets opening on high streets. Although they are more expensive than regular supermarkets, you can be sure that all the produce has been carefully sourced from high-quality organic suppliers.

READ THE LABEL

When shopping for food, always read the label carefully (*see pages 96–97*). Select items that are low in or free from additives and preservatives and synthetic food colourants, are not highly packaged, or are packaged in recyclable material such as paper rather than plastic. Ask for unbleached coffee filters, tissues, toilet paper,

and nappies that are chlorine-free. Consumer demand is making these products much more common.

Demand for unusual varieties of popular fruits and vegetables (here, sprouting broccoli) ensure biodiversity.

SHOPPING FOR SEASONAL FRUITS AND VEGETABLES

Generally speaking, you will get the best flavour when buying in season. This at-a-glance table will help you see the best time of year to buy certain fruit and vegetables to ensure that they are fresh: there will be variations according to local produce in particular climates, and in some cases produce may be imported.

WINTER	Cauliflower	Chinese leaves	Sweet peppers
Beetroot	Chicory	Courgettes	Sweetcorn
Brussels' sprouts	Cress	Cucumber	Tomatoes
Cabbage	Mushrooms	French beans	
Cauliflower	New potatoes	Garlic	**AUTUMN**
Celery and celeriac	Radishes	Herbs (most at their	Apples
Jerusalem artichokes	Shallots	best in early summer)	Beetroot
Leeks	Sorrel	Lamb's lettuce	Broccoli
Onions		Lettuce	Brussels' sprouts
Parsnips	**SUMMER**	New potatoes	Cabbage
Potatoes	Apples	Peaches	Celery and celeriac
Swedes	Apricots	Peas	Fennel
Winter squash	Artichokes	Mangetout	Marrow
	Broad beans	Plums	Pears
SPRING	Carrots	Runner beans	Plums
Artichokes	Cauliflower	Soft berries	Spinach
Asparagus	Cherries	Spinach	Squashes

FOOD PACKAGING

In spite of the fact that it is a legal requirement that packaging should not harm health or affect food quality, the following information points out where packaging issues are still a problem.

LEAD-SOLDERED CANS

Although lead-soldered cans for food have been phased out in most countries, lead-soldered cans may be imported from countries that still use them. These cans are easy to recognize because they have a top and bottom rim, and a soldered side seam that has small dents along it. (Lead-free cans are either seamless or welded with a dark paint line along the seam.) The lead leaches into the food, which can lead to neurological damage. Behavioural problems in children, such as hyperactivity, have been linked to lead in food.

Fresh produce bought direct from the supplier is not sealed in plastic, which has health and packaging advantages.

PLASTIC PACKAGING

Plastic-coated cans may leach plastic molecules into the foods they contain, while processed foods are frequently packaged in layers of plastic. Chemicals in some plastics may also migrate into food when heated, which is often the case with microwave convenience foods. The health effects of plastic residues in food are unknown.

CHOOSING WINES & BEER

There is evidence that moderate amounts of wine and beer are good for your health, and may help to prevent heart disease and strokes. However, as with food, non-organic wines and beers may contain a range of additives and contaminants.

WINE
● There is no legal requirement to list the ingredients that go into wine, so it is a good idea to choose brands that voluntarily do so.
● Wines themselves often contain anything up to 20 additives to enhance their taste, flavour, and colour.
● The sulphites sometimes added to inhibit oxidation and spoilage in non-organic wines can cause allergic reactions. However, sulphite is formed naturally during the fermentation process, so it cannot be avoided completely.
● Grapes for non-organic wine-making are commonly treated with about a dozen applications of pesticides in the growing season. Buying wine made with organic grapes ensures a pesticide-free product.
● Organic vineyards maintain a healthy balance in the soil.
● Biodynamic viticulture is an organic approach that uses special homeopathic sprays and the movements of the planets in the cultivation process.

BEER
● As with wines, non-organic beers are made from hops sprayed with chemicals, and have artificial flavourings and colourings added.
● Organic beers are available. Some are additive-free, and will be labelled as such.
● Buying locally brewed draught beer saves on the transportation, processing, and bottling that bottled beers undergo.
● Try brewing your own beer. It is fun and saves money.

PLANNING YOUR SHOPPING

The following tips are intended to help you plan your shopping trips more efficiently and help build up a storecupboard of essential items so that you do not have to expend unnecessary energy making wasted journeys.

● Buy non-perishable goods in bulk: rice, pulses, pasta, flour, and seeds, toilet paper, canned foods, and cleaning products all fall into this category. Bulk-buying cuts down on packaging, saves money, and reduces the number of shopping trips you make.
● Make sure dried foods are stored in a cool, dry, pest-free environment to keep them in good condition.
● Keep a running shopping list, adding to it when you are aware that items are getting low. Make sure that all your family is involved in this to make managing the household simpler. Using a shopping list means that you will not be tempted to buy foods that you don't need, which will cut down on wastage.
● Some perishable goods such as bread, milk, and butter can be frozen, so store them in bulk in the freezer. Freezing sliced bread keeps it fresh, and you can remove it one slice at a time for toasting.
● Consider sharing trips to the supermarket with a friend – it will halve your fuel costs as well as reducing pollution.

Essential cooking ingredients such as flour can be stored in bulk. Once opened, store in an airtight glass jar.

WILD FOODS

Throughout the year it is possible to gather wild produce from many natural habitats, and so make the most of "food for free".

● A suitable field guide to wild plants will help you to find and identify the many edible herbs and leafy plants that can be harvested wild. In autumn, make the most of fruits and nuts that grow wild in fields, hedgerows, and woodland.
● Pick wild foods from hedgerows and verges as far away from main roads as possible, to avoid contamination from petrol fumes.
● If you are unsure that you have correctly identified a wild food, it is best to leave the plant alone. Some wild plants are poisonous.
● Collect only what you can reasonably use yourself – do not strip an area of its crop – and always check if you need to ask permission first.

Always check with an expert before eating any wild mushrooms you have found. Chanterelle mushrooms, shown here, are safe to eat, and are easy to identify by their distinctive yellow gills.

PREPARING FOOD

The kitchen is at the heart of the home, and keeping it clean and fresh the natural way is paramount. As well as ensuring basic cleanliness, there are many common sense and natural tips for hygienic food preparation that will create a safe environment and avoid the health risks associated with contamination. Bacteria can contaminate all kinds of foods, causing violent stomach upsets, diarrhoea, vomiting, and headaches, and sometimes more acute illness.

If **wooden worktops** become pungent, rub them with a cut lemon and the odour will disappear.

KEEPING THE KITCHEN CLEAN

A clean, tidy kitchen is not only desirable for health, but also creates a more pleasant environment in which to enjoy cooking. To ensure basic kitchen hygiene, follow the simple guidelines below.

- Keep your kitchen free of houseflies and other insects (*see pages 60–61*).
- Avoid open shelving: it attracts dust. Keep kitchen equipment in cupboards and drawers.
- Keep pets off work surfaces and tables: they carry bacteria that can spread disease.
- Reserve the kitchen sink for chores connected with food only: germs left in the sink from clearing up household mess can easily contaminate food.
- Use separate cloths for different purposes to avoid cross-contamination: floor cloths should not be used to clean kitchen surfaces, tea-towels are for drying dishes, and towels for hands.
- A dishwasher gets dishes cleaner and sanitizes them. It is also more economical with water than handwashing.
- Clean out your oven and hob, refrigerator and freezer regularly (*see page 53*).
- Dispose of kitchen waste regularly. Empty it as often as you need to, and sprinkle a little baking soda into the waste bin to reduce odours.

HANDLING FOOD

Maintaining adequate hygiene while handling food is crucial in preventing food-borne infections. There is nothing difficult about good hygiene practices – most are just common sense. Get into the habit of following them, and you will find they soon become second nature.

Leave hand-washed glasses to dry naturally on a clean cloth. This is more hygienic than wiping them dry.

PREPARATION

- If you have cuts or scratches on your hands, use rubber gloves while preparing foods, to stop bacteria from your wounds from contaminating the food.
- Always wash your hands with hot water and soap and dry them thoroughly on a clean towel before handling food.
- Wash all fruit and vegetables: rinse or scrub under running water before use, especially if they have been grown with pesticides and fertilizers.
- Where the food type allows, cook food from frozen rather than defrosting it to reduce the health risk of bacteria spreading during the defrosting process.
- Clean up kitchen work surfaces as you cook to keep food preparation areas as hygienic as possible.

COOKING

- Cook foods at as high a temperature as possible, and for an adequate length of time, to neutralize harmful bacteria. The same applies to reheating leftovers.
- Always cook meat thoroughly, until the juices run clear (use a thermometer if you are unsure, or according to the instructions in a good cookery book).

Thaw frozen foods in the refrigerator rather than at room temperature to prevent bacteria from multiplying.

SAFE COOKING: POTS & PANS

Use glass or terracotta dishes, and cast iron, porcelain-enamel coated, or anodized aluminium pans. Foods cooked in aluminium react with it to form aluminium salts, which dissolve when exposed to acids, such as those in tomatoes. These salts have been connected with Alzheimer's disease, dementia, and impaired motor-visual co-ordination. The anodizing process seals aluminium by dipping it into a hot acid bath. Stainless steel may leach toxic metals such as chromium or nickel, and scratched plastic-coated pans should not be used because they contaminate food with plastic molecules.

REFRIGERATING & FREEZING

- Keep the refrigerator temperature at around 4°C (39°F), and your freezer at -18°C (0.3°F). When opening a compartment door, do so for as short a time as possible to stop cold air from escaping, and to save energy.
- Chill or freeze food rapidly, in small quantities.
- The door of the fridge is the least cold part, so do not store meat or dairy produce there.

Instead, use it for opened pickle jars, soft drinks and wine, and jams.
- Fresh food should be refrigerated as soon as possible after buying to prevent any existing bacteria from multiplying. The exception is fruit, which needs to be left out to ripen, and gourmet cheeses, whose bacterial activity (and flavour) is killed off by refrigeration.

CLEARING-UP & LEFTOVER FOOD

- Thoroughly clean chopping boards after use, to prevent cross-contamination between meat, fish, vegetables, and fruit. Use a natural surface cleaner (*see page 52*), or rub with a cut lemon. To be extra safe, use different chopping boards and utensils for meat, fish, and vegetables or fruit.
- Chill leftovers immediately: botulism can develop if cooked food is allowed to remain at room temperature overnight – as could happen with, say, a slightly warm, leftover baked potato, or vegetables wrapped tightly in foil.

PERSONAL CARE

Personal care products based on natural and – increasingly – organic ingredients constitute an expanding segment of the beauty market. People are more aware than ever of health issues, animal rights, and environmental concerns when buying cosmetics and toiletries.

PRODUCT MANUFACTURE

The beauty industry is big business and every year 100,000 tons of chemicals are used to make products. Most cosmetics contain additives and preservatives, and they may also include genetically modified ingredients. Some of these contents may be absorbed directly into the bloodstream through the skin during application, and then accumulate in the body tissue. Over 99 per cent of oils used in cosmetics are based on petrochemicals, or on chemically extracted and refined plant oils that have been bleached and deodorized, their vitamins removed. There is increasingly convincing evidence that regular long-term applications of such products can constitute a potentially serious health risk.

NATURAL BEAUTY

Often, the legal requirement is that products can be labelled "natural" provided at least 1 per cent of their ingredients are from natural sources. Ingredients are often listed in small print, or even sealed inside the packaging, so that they cannot be read before you buy the product. You do not have to buy all your beauty care items, however: to be really sure of what you are putting on your body, there are simple ways of making your own products with pure and natural ingredients.

Toothpastes made with natural ingredients such as fennel and eucalyptus are now available.

Natural skin treats p116

Body care p119

Foot cream recipe p123

Natural deodorants p125

UNDERSTANDING LABELS

The cosmetics and toiletries industry is only partially regulated. The European Union prohibits the use of over 700 ingredients, while the INCI (International Nomenclature of Cosmetic Ingredients) lists restricted chemicals, yet of the 3,000 registered chemicals companies may legally use in their products, only limited research has been carried out on many of them. Furthermore, legislation on labelling is not universal, and does not apply to some soaps, toothpastes, deodorants, sunscreens, and shampoos. American law requires that the ingredients, but not the finished cosmetic product, be tested for safety before they are released to the marketplace.

CHEMICALS TO AVOID

The following ingredients found in beauty products are best avoided or used only occasionally. Check the product label first before buying or using.

Check the contents of soaps before purchase – many contain artificial fragrances, colours, and preservatives.

PETROCHEMICAL-BASED PRODUCTS
Products based on petrochemicals are widely used in cosmetics. Mineral oils, petrolatum (also known as mineral oil jelly), paraffin, and any ingredient that has the prefix propyl-, methyl-, or ethe- are used in products to "hydrate" the skin. However, because they cannot be absorbed through the skin but sit on the surface, in the process they block the skin's natural function of respiration, inhibiting its ability to eliminate toxins. Petrolatum may cause drying and premature ageing of the skin, and strip the skin of its lubricating oils. Propylene glycol is used to improve foundations and moisturizers: it is also found in anti-freeze. It is known to cause cancer in rats. Benzyl alcohol (used in both ballpoint pens and perfume) is an irritant to skin and mucous membranes.

SODIUM LAURYL SULPHATE (SLS)
This detergent and foaming agent is found in engine degreasers and harsh cleansing solutions. It is used in bath and shower gels and shampoos, cleansers, and most toothpastes. It can cause skin rashes, hair loss, and eye damage.

DEA, TEA, & MEA
Diethanolaminooleamide, triethanolamine, and monoethanolamine are ammonia derivatives found in foams, shower gels, body lotions, moisturizers, and facial cleaners. Their chemical function is to bind oil and water together and act as detergents. They are known allergens.

PPD
Paraphenylene-diamine, used to produce the black colour in hair dyes, can cause allergic reactions and is linked to certain cancers.

Most natural toothpastes do not use sodium lauryl sulphate, a foaming agent that is an irritant to mucous membranes.

PARABENS

Methylparaben and propylparaben are petrochemical-based preservatives used to extend the shelf-life of water-based products and inhibit bacterial growth. They are irritants, yet are found in virtually all toiletries, some toothpastes, and deodorants. They mimic oestrogens and have been linked to breast and testicular cancer, prostate disorders, and sperm abnormalities.

FORMALDEHYDE

This prevalent chemical toxin is found in cosmetic preservatives. As a cosmetic ingredient, it is not easy to recognize, since it is associated with the additives 2-bromo-2-nitropropane, 3-diol Diazolidinyl urea, DMDM hydantoin, or Quaternium-15. It is widely used in shampoos and handwashes, and some nail hardeners. In Sweden and Japan, its use in cosmetics has been banned.

Organic or homemade creams and lotions avoid the use of potentially harmful synthetic ingredients.

DBP & DEP

Dibutylphthalate and diethylphthalate are toxic and highly allergenic chemicals that cause birth defects in rats, yet may be used in skin creams to enhance absorption and as emollients and humidifiers. In nail polish and mascara, they are used to create a flexible film.

ARTIFICIAL COLOURS

Known as FD&C Blue 1, Green 3, D&C Red 33, and FD&C Yellow 5 and 6, these artificial colours are potential carcinogens and can damage blood platelets and bone marrow. Carmine can cause allergic reactions.

KATHON GC

This preservative is thought to damage cell growth in ways that may lead to cancer. It is often found listed on shampoos and hair conditioners.

AHAs & BHAs

Alpha-hydroxy acids and beta-hydroxy acids are used as moisturizers in skin creams, dandruff shampoos, and foundations with sunscreens. Little research has been done on them, but they are suspected of increasing cell turnover and decreasing the thickness of the outer skin, making it more sensitive to the sun's rays.

LANOLIN

Although this natural emollient for softening and moisturizing the skin derives from sheep's wool, it can be contaminated in its cosmetic grade. Known contaminants include pesticides such as DDT, lindane, and dieldrin. Creams and lipsticks with lanolin can cause acne.

UNDERSTAND THE JARGON

• "Natural" has no legal or scientific definition. To be labelled as such, a product need contain only 1 per cent natural ingredients.
• "Naturally inspired" is equally unspecific.
• "Organic" is the only definition that actually means "chemical-free".
• "Hypoallergenic" is an equally meaningless term because allergies are individual: what this actually means is that the most common allergens, such as fragrance, lanolin, cocoa butter, cornstarch, and cottonseed oils, are removed from the product.
• "Dermatologically tested" has no approved definition and may mean sanctioned by a dermatologist with no national or legal recognition.

PERSULPHATE SALTS

These act as boosting agents in hair bleaches and have been linked to occupational asthma among hairdressers. They may also be present in over-the-counter bleaching products.

CHEMICAL UV FILTERS

Sunscreen chemicals such as octyl methoxycinnamate and octyl dimethyl PABA can cause allergic reactions, eczema, rashes, and swellings and may contribute to skin ageing.

ARTIFICIAL FRAGRANCES

(*see page 124*)

SKIN CARE

About 60 per cent of any substance applied directly to the skin surface is readily absorbed, so our bodies may take in up to 2kg (4.4lb) chemicals every year through this largest organ of the body. Since the effects of many of the chemicals added to toiletries and cosmetics are either unknown or toxic, it makes sense to use skin care products that are derived from natural ingredients. Many organic beauty products use only natural pigments and preservatives, and natural oils from plants grown without pesticides or artificial fertilizers (*see Resources page 170*).

Fragrance-free, natural skin cream is available from good health shops. Add a few drops of essential oil to scent it.

IS IT NATURAL?

Most of us are familiar with natural beauty ingredients such as almond oil, witch hazel, and rose water. However, the labels of natural products often list more mysterious items such as capyrlic or capric triglyceride. Equally, some people may be concerned about using products derived from animal sources. Certain items, such as glycerine or stearic acid, may come from either an animal or a plant source.

ALLANTOIN
A by-product of uric acid obtained from animals. A plant-based alternative is made from comfrey root; it protects, softens, and heals.

COCONUT DERIVATIVES
The coconut is a rich source of ingredients for natural skin care products. Coconut-based cleansers include cocomide DEA, cocamidopropyl betaine, and glyceryl cocate. Many animal-derived ingredients can also be made from coconut. These include the emulsifier and emollients caprylic/capric triglyceride, cetyl alcohol, and cetearyl alcohol.

EMULSIFYING WAX
A wax used to disperse the oil and water in ointments. This is usually made from animal fats, but vegetable-derived forms are available.

GLYCERINE
Obtained from oils and fats, this is an excellent moisturizer and emollient. Vegetable glycerine is available, but most is made from animal fat as a by-product of soap manufacture. Glyceryl stearate is derived from glycerine and stearic acid (*see opposite*). It is used in beauty products to soothe and soften, and is an effective emulsifier.

POTASSIUM SORBATE
Also known as K-sorbate, this plant-based preservative is derived from sorbic acid and is used in small amounts as an anti-microbial and anti-fungal agent in cosmetics.

SODIUM BENZOATE
A food-grade preservative that occurs naturally in many plants. It is also antiseptic.

STEARIC ACID
This is most commonly derived from the fat of sheep or cattle, but a vegetable source from the palm or coconut is also available. It soothes, softens, and emulsifies. Stearyl alcohol is prepared from cetyl alcohol and stearic acid and fulfils a similar emulsifying role.

TOCOPHEROL
Commonly known as vitamin E, this antioxidant fights free radicals and improves skin condition. It also acts as a natural preservative. It may appear on the label as D-alpha tocopherol.

IMPROVING SKIN CONDITION

For a naturally healthy complexion, you do not have to resort to a cocktail of products. Enjoying a good diet rich in fresh fruit and vegetables, drinking plenty of water, taking regular exercise, and sleeping well all do wonders for improving the tone and appearance of the skin. Simply follow the guidelines outlined below.

- Follow a healthy diet of fresh organic ingredients (*see pages 90–91*) to give the skin the nutrients and natural oils on which it thrives.
- Take regular, moderate exercise – just brisk walking several times a week in the fresh air makes a substantial difference to your circulation and metabolism, improving the appearance of the skin.
- Do facial exercises: tensing and relaxing cheek muscles helps to improve skin tone.
- Try meditation, relaxation, and breathing exercises to relax the face and oxygenate the bloodstream.
- Don't underestimate the benefits of regular, restful sleep. Get plenty of it.
- Buy natural oils and skin care products based on 100 per cent organic ingredients.
- Don't smoke: cigarettes dehydrate the skin and encourage wrinkles.
- Avoid excess alcohol – it dehydrates the skin, strips cells of vital moisture and causes premature ageing.
- Avoid too much caffeine, which depletes the skin of some vitamins and minerals.
- Excess salt will overload the kidneys and lead to fluid retention. It can contribute to dark circles under the eyes and cellulite on the arms and legs.
- Skin blemishes and disorders such as acne are often linked to a diet too rich in refined sugar.
- Avoid petroleum-based mineral oil products, which may dry out the skin.
- Get away from the city when possible: man-made chemicals in urban and industrial areas pollute the skin and body as well as the environment.

Drink plenty of filtered water (*see page 99*), about 1 litre (¾ pints) a day. Human beings are made up of over 70 per cent water, and the skin is the largest organ of the body. It is thirsty.

Natural lipsticks are free of chemical colouring pigments and fragrances, and are available with ingredients such as beeswax, mineral pigments, and essential oils.

MAKE-UP FOR HEALTH

Perhaps the most toxic of all cosmetic products is lipstick, because it is applied regularly to the thinner skin on the lips and so is easily absorbed. Commercially produced lipsticks may contain PVP (polyvinylpyrrolidone), saccharin, and artificial colours and fragrances (*see page 124*).

Mascara can also be a problem as it may contain formaldehyde, alcohol, DBP, and some plastic resins that can cause irritation, redness, burning, and swelling. Foundation usually contains artificial colours and fragrances. Buy make-up made with natural mineral pigments and organic materials (*see Resources page 170*).

A whole range of fresh, edible ingredients from your kitchen storecupboard and refrigerator can be used to make natural and effective beauty treatments that are free of chemicals.

- Use plain natural organic yogurt as a daily skin cleanser. Apply with your fingertips, then rinse off with lukewarm water.
- Organic apple cider vinegar makes a superb skin toner. Moisten a cotton pad with vinegar and dab it onto the skin. Rinse with water.
- Rose water also makes a good skin toner, especially for mature skins. Moisten a cotton pad and dab the rose water on to the skin.
- Mix equal parts of vegetable glycerine, available from most chemists, and water, for a beautifully softening skin moisturizer.
- Buy pure, untreated organic lanolin from a natural health shop and apply a small amount to dry skin once or twice a week: this rich oil is extracted from sheep's wool and nourishes the skin. Some people are mildly allergic to lanolin, so do not continue to use it if you find that it irritates your skin.
- If your skin is very dry, dab pure almond oil, or peach, avocado, or even a light olive oil on to the face at least once or twice a week. This will replenish the skin's natural oils and soften and moisturize it.
- Cut the top off a capsule of vitamin E and apply to the delicate skin under the eyes to soften and smooth it. This can be used at night or in the morning.

Apple cider vinegar, rose water, almond oil, vegetable glycerine, avocado, green clay, and yogurt are all you need to keep your skin clean, soft, and supple.

REGENERATING GREEN CLAY MASK

Green clay (*see Resources page 170*) is one of nature's best ingredients for a facial: this bio-mineral is a powerful agent of regeneration and leaves the skin feeling elastic, enriched, and fresh. Simply mix 2 tablespoons of green clay powder with enough filtered water to produce a smooth, creamy consistency. Apply the clay all over your face, and lie down to rest and to allow the nutrients to sink deeply into the skin. After 10–15 minutes, the clay will have set hard. Wipe it off gently with a soft damp sponge, and dab the skin with rose water on a cotton wool pad. Afterwards, apply a natural oil if your skin needs moisturizing. Use this natural regenerating treatment once or twice a month.

STEAM FACIAL
This is excellent for deep-cleansing the skin. Stir in a handful of dried herbs – calendula, chamomile, lavender, and rosemary are all good for the skin – to a bowl of hot water. Sit over the bowl with a towel over your head for about 5 minutes, then splash your face with cool water.

AVOCADO FACIAL

This leaves your face feeling wonderfully soft and refreshed.

YOU WILL NEED
2 tbs avocado
1 tsp runny honey
3–4 drops cider vinegar

Wrap a towel around your shoulders to protect your clothes, and tie back your hair to keep it off your face. Apply the mixture, avoiding the area around the eyes, and lie down for about 10–15 minutes to allow the mask to soak in and work. Then wipe off with a soft, damp cloth, rinse gently in warm water, and apply some rose water as a finishing touch to soften and smooth the skin.

1 Cut the avocado flesh into small pieces, and place in a bowl. Stir in the honey, then add the vinegar.

2 Mash the mixture with a fork until you have a creamy, smooth paste. Apply it to your face for 10–15 minutes.

OUT IN THE SUN

Getting enough sunshine is essential for physical and mental health as it aids the production of vitamin D: studies show that women who live in sunnier climates have 30-40 per cent less breast cancer than those in northern regions, and that those who remain indoors out of the sun are also more likely to develop breast cancer than sun-loving women. However, on the down side, it is generally agreed that over-exposure to strong sunlight can increase the risk of skin cancer. Research is continuing into the efficacy of sunscreens, but there is serious evidence that they may only protect against basal-cell or squamous cell carcinomas, and they may also contribute to the ageing of the skin. Some sunscreens contain chemicals that mimic the effects of oestrogens and have caused developmental problems in rats.

NATURAL SUNSCREENS

● Taking vitamin C (2 grams per day) and vitamin E (1000 iu per day) may help protect against sunburn, according to the American Academy of Dermatology.

● Look for products that contain the UV filter oryzanol, which occurs naturally in rice-bran and has enough UV absorption to be usefully incorporated into skincare products. It is further potentiated by the addition of vitamin E to the product and can offer some UV protection. It is also a known antioxidant. (*See Resources page 170.*)

● People with the lightest skin, hair, and eyes are at greatest risk of contracting skin cancers, so if that applies to you, don't expose yourself to the sun for long periods.

Wear a hat or a scarf in strong sun, or stay in the shade.

● If you get sunburnt, mix up a solution of baking soda and water to make a thin paste and dab on to the affected parts.

● Although a certain amount of sunshine is good for you, you should avoid exposure between 10am and 4pm during the summer months, when the sun is at its strongest.

BODY CARE

You can avoid the hazards linked to the chemical constituents in "off-the-shelf" products for body care and personal hygiene by buying the natural organic alternatives that are now available (*see Resources page 170*). You can also make your baths and showers luxurious and aromatic using natural ingredients that are chemical-free, cost very little, and have no adverse impact on the environment. To complete the experience, use unbleached cotton towels and bathmats, and soft towelling robes – then take time out to pamper yourself.

BATHS & SHOWERS

Bathing is not just about keeping clean. The whole ritual can be healing, calming and rejuvenating, especially with the help of the right natural products.

BATHING SUGGESTIONS

The basic constituents of bubble bath are detergent and artificial fragrance. These ingredients may cause skin irritations and even vaginal and urinary tract infections. Here are some fragrant and relaxing natural alternatives to add to your bath water:

● 2 litres (3½ pints) organic whole milk or buttermilk (Cleopatra's recipe for a perfect skin).

● A dash of olive oil, almond oil or avocado oil, plus up to 5 drops fragrant essential oils or a mixture of your favourite natural fragrances, to create whatever mood you want (see pages 124–125 for essential oil ideas).

● 1 cup Epsom salts (not more than twice a week), to soften the skin beautifully and gently detoxify the body.

● A few slices of lemon to soften and bleach the skin.

● A handful of fragrant dried herbs and spices (lavender, rosemary, bay, marjoram, cloves, cardamom, allspice, cinnamon) tied in a muslin bag and soaked in the hot water to give out a fabulous fragrance.

Make your own bath oil by adding essential oils to a vegetable oil base (about 6 drops per 1 tablespoon), mixing together well. Pour into the bath and agitate the water to disperse.

SOAP

Soap is not considered to be a cosmetic, so manufacturers are not required to list its ingredients. Basic soap is usually made from animal fats, lye (sodium hydroxide), and glycerine. "Antibacterial" and "deodorant" soaps, however, can contain a host of harmful chemicals, including triclosan. Soaps may contain artificial fragrances, colours, and preservatives. Vegetable-based soaps are your best bet. They are widely available and will be clearly labelled. They are plain, unscented, and uncoloured, and made from natural vegetable sources such as olive or almond oil, or vegetable glycerine.

AFTER-BATH TREATS

● To moisturize dry skin, apply a small amount of oil such as sweet almond or apricot kernel oil. Scent with a few drops of essential oil.

● For a refreshing body splash, add 3 tsp aloe vera gel, 3 tsp witch hazel, and 5 drops essential oil of your choice to 100ml (4fl oz) spring water in an atomizer. Shake before use. If you store in a cool place, it should keep for about two weeks.

● Try mixing orris root and cornstarch in equal parts for an effective natural talc (*see page 123*).

ORAL CARE

Some toothpastes contain fluoride, sodium lauryl sulphate, PVP, saccharin, artificial flavourings, and colourings. Mouthwashes often contain ethanol, artificial colours, and ammonia, and may be labelled unsafe to swallow. For natural dental hygiene try:

● Baking soda – a dentist-approved tooth cleaner and a good plaque-fighter.

● Toothpastes based on natural ingredients that are chemical-free (*see Resources page 170*).

● Cold mint tea as a mouthwash.

Treat yourself to organic cotton towels and bathmats, and towelling robes that contain no chemical dyes.

COTTON WOOL, TOILET PAPER, AND TISSUES

Formaldehyde, artificial fragrance, and dyes are all present in many brands of toilet paper, which are also likely to have been bleached with chlorine and to contain dioxins, a family of toxic chemicals. Coloured toilet paper contain dyes based on artificial colours. Try to avoid these products and go for the following alternatives instead.

• Choose recycled toilet paper and organic cotton wool that are dioxin-safe and chemical-free (*see Resources page 170*).

• Try to buy unscented, undyed, unbleached facial tissues.

FEMININE HYGIENE

Ever since Toxic Shock Syndrome was linked to tampons, the use of certain rayons and polyesters has been banned. However, viscose rayon is still used in tampons and opinion is divided as to its toxic effect. The sterile whiteness of sanitary products may be deceptively reassuring because chlorine bleaching releases organochlorines such as dioxins. An alternative process, elemental chlorine-free bleaching (ECF), while safer, may still release minute traces of dioxins.

BUYING FEMININE HYGIENE PRODUCTS

● Purchase tampons labelled "no superabsorbent fibres".

● Use certified biodegradable organic cotton tampons, unbleached – or, as a second-best option, bleached using a chlorine-free method.

● Use sanitary pads instead of tampons, buying natural, organic, unbleached, non-perfumed varieties without plastic backings because these do not biodegrade (*see Resources page 170*).

● Try to find reusable cotton pads, which are becoming more widely available (*see Resources page 170*).

HAIR CARE

There are many chemical ingredients – often unlisted and sometimes not fully tested – in hair care products, so it is wise to buy organic, or to make your own shampoos, conditioners, and rinses using food ingredients such as lemon, cider vinegar, eggs, and herbs such as soapwort and lemon verbena. If you have permed or coloured hair, make sure that your stylist uses ammonia-free products.

SHAMPOOS & CONDITIONERS

Commercial shampoos often contain Quaternium-15, which releases formaldehyde, and sodium lauryl sulphate (*see pages 112–113*). Dandruff shampoos can be particularly problematic, and may include selenium sulphide (linked to damage of internal organs) or resorcinol (may cause irritation to the eyes and skin). Shampoos may also contain the liquid plastic polymer PVP, detergents, and artificial colours and fragrances. Use an organic shampoo based on plant materials, or try the following alternatives.

NATURAL HEAD LICE TREATMENT

Head lice infestation is common among children: however, prescription products and over-the-counter remedies rely on highly toxic pesticides. Instead, use an olive, neem, or coconut oil shampoo – these oils kill lice. Rinse with hot water, shampoo a second time, rinse again, then comb out the hair with a nit comb, rinsing out the comb in a jug of hot water after each sweep. Give the hair a final rinse in a bowl of hot water and cider vinegar (1 litre/2 pints water to 230ml/8fl oz vinegar.) Dry the hair, then check it again. Remove remaining nits or eggs with double-sided tape or tweezers. Repeat twice a week until the infestation has gone.

Brushing the hair stimulates the scalp and massages it at the same time. Choose a brush that is gentle on the scalp for best results.

● Instead of using shampoo, beat an egg and massage it into the scalp. Rinse in warm water, and use the juice of half a lemon in the final rinse for added shine.
● If you suffer from dandruff, massage pure apple juice into the scalp, leave for several minutes, then rinse off. Or mix

SOAPWORT SHAMPOO

This is suitable for all hair types. Soapwort (*Saponaria officinalis*) contains saponins, which produce a lather similar to soap. Lemon verbena gives this shampoo a delicious citrus fragrance and catnip promotes healthy hair growth. This recipe makes enough for 6–7 shampoos, and keeps 8–10 days if stored in a cool, dark place.

2 teaspoons of cider vinegar in 1 cup water and massage in.
● Rub baking soda into wet hair after shampooing, massaging it in well. Rinse out. Baking soda makes a fabulous conditioner, leaving your hair beautifully soft.
● Add cider vinegar to the final rinse to add shine.

YOU WILL NEED:
1½ tbsp dried soapwort root, chopped
450 ml (15 fl oz) water
2 tsp dried lemon verbena
2 tsp dried catnip

Simmer the soapwort in water for 20 minutes. Remove from the heat, add the herbs, and cool. Strain into a bottle.

NATURAL LEMON HAIR SPRAY

Hair sprays and mousses may contain the plastic polymer PVP, formaldehyde, artificial fragrance, and alcohol, which can cause skin reactions and irritation to both the eyes and nose. Sprays may contain aerosol propellants using CFCs that damage the ozone layer. The following recipe offers a natural alternative:

YOU WILL NEED
1 lemon (or 1 orange if hair
   is very dry), chopped
450ml (15fl oz) water
1 tbsp vodka

This natural hair spray relies on vodka as a preservative, which gives it a shelf-life of up to four weeks. If you keep it in the refrigerator, it should last a little longer. The spray leaves your hair feeling soft and smelling aromatic, as well as keeping it in place. For flyaway hair, you could also try an infusion of dried rosemary. Add a dessertspoon of the herb to the same amount of water and simmer for 10 minutes, then strain, cool, and use.

1 Place the lemon and the water in a saucepan and bring to the boil. Simmer until reduced by half. Cool, then strain.

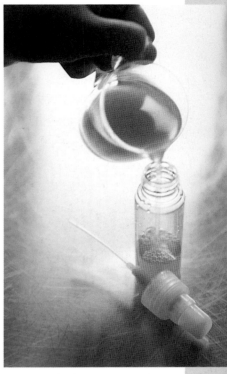

2 Add the vodka to the mixture to preserve it, then pour into a fine spray bottle and store in a cool place.

HAIR COLOURINGS

Research into hair dyes is ongoing. In 2001, a study by the University of Southern California found that women who use permanent dyes at least once a month for one year or longer were more at risk of bladder cancer than normal. Earlier studies have found that long-serving hairstylists ran three times the normal risk of bladder and breast cancers after working with chemical hair dyes. Dark-coloured, permanent dyes have been singled out for particular concern. Manufactured hair dyes are known to contain up to 20 chemicals, some of which have not been fully tested for safety and are exempt from legislation. Try these natural hair colourants instead.

● Organic hair colourings based on plant ingredients such as marigold, hibiscus, indigo, and henna are available, so seek out a hair stylist who uses them.
● Use henna to darken or highlight hair, but make sure that it is "pure".
● Have highlights ("foils") put into your hair instead of full hair colour: this way the dye does not touch the scalp and penetrate the skin.
● Cold black tea and coffee make wonderful hair rinses for dark hair, both to strengthen colour and to hide grey hairs. In a large bowl, pour 600 ml (1 pint) of boiling water over 3 teabags or 3 tablespoons of coffee grounds and leave until cold. Strain off and keep in the refrigerator, where it will keep for up to two weeks. Apply to dry hair and allow to dry. Reapply after each wash.
● Cold chamomile tea can be used in a similar way to black tea to highlight blonde hair.

HAND & FOOT CARE

The fashionable emphasis on manicures and pedicures in recent years has brought more people into frequent contact with numerous harsh chemicals found in nail varnishes and nail varnish remover, many of which pose health problems. Ideally, learn to love your hands and feet in their natural state, saving painted nails for special occasions. Use the suggestions here to promote naturally soft skin and healthy, shiny nails.

NATURAL HAND CARE

It is a fairly straightforward process to make your own moisturizing hand oil or to find products in organic supermarkets and health shops made from organic natural ingredients (*see Resources page 170*). Here are some homemade recipes to try out.

- Add a dash of almond oil or even plain olive oil to a basin of water when you wash your hands, to soften them.
- Massage a few drops of almond oil into dry hands.
- For a scented oil, add a few drops of patchouli, lemon, and lavender essential oil to a 60ml bottle of almond or jojoba oil.
- Mix equal quantities of coconut oil and vegetable glycerine in a small bottle and rub well into your hands.
- Mix 1 teaspoon honey with 2 teaspoons almond oil or olive oil and add 2 drops of lemon essential oil. Rub in well.

NAIL VARNISH

The problem with nail varnish is that many contain harmful chemicals such as toluene and other solvents, as well as formaldehyde resin. These substances may cause nose and throat irritations, rashes, headaches, nausea, and asthma. The worst allergic reactions are caused by the plasticizer dibutyl phthalate (DBP), which is known to cause birth defects in animals, and is especially dangerous to the male reproductive system. It is used as a coating agent in nail polishes, topcoats, and hardeners to prevent the polish from cracking, but it leaches into your skin whenever you wash your hands. In addition, nail varnish remover contains acetone, a powerful solvent derived from petroleum. To limit your exposure to these chemicals, follow the guidelines below.

- Buy nail products that avoid these chemicals (*see Resources page 170*).
- If you use nail colour on your toenails, use a safe water-based paint, or a varnish containing as few chemicals as possible (*see Resources page 170*).
- Avoid nail hardeners and strengthen your nails and stimulate the circulation by rubbing in walnut, almond, or neem oil, scented with one or two drops of frankincense. This is also an effective cuticle softener: after massaging it in, just ease the cuticles back.

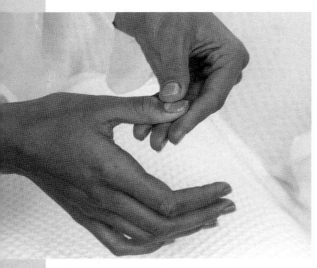

Bring a natural shine to nails by applying a small amount of vegetable or neem oil, then buffing with a nail buffer.

NATURAL FOOT CARE

Feet are often neglected and respond well to a little pampering. Caring for your feet couldn't be simpler if you use the natural products described here.

● Remove rough or dead skin by rubbing with pumice stone (natural volcanic silicate).
● Massage small amounts of almond oil into toenails to strengthen them and keep them from drying out.
● Treat your feet to an occasional refreshing massage with 20ml (1 tablespoon) almond oil mixed with 6 drops of peppermint essential oil.

FOOT CREAM

This light, scented cream will keep for about six months if stored in a cool, dark place.

YOU WILL NEED

50g (2oz) natural cream base
   (see Resources page 170)
6 drops apricot kernel oil
6 drops frankincense
   essential oil
6 drops geranium essential oil
6 drops benzoin essential oil

The cream and apricot oil will moisturize the feet and prevent the dry skin, while the essential oils add fragrance.

1 Place the natural cream base in a bowl and add 6 drops each of the essential oils.

2 Whisk together with a small wooden spatula and transfer into a small glass container with a sealed lid.

3 Massage the cream into the feet after a bath, while the skin is still damp.

TALCUM POWDER

Some people like to apply talcum powder to their feet after bathing. Talc is made from magnesium trisilicate, a mineral obtained from the mining of talc rocks. It contains minute fibres that are easily inhaled, and is closely related in structure to asbestos. A 1993 National Toxicology programme carried out in the United States showed that talc caused tumours in the ovaries and lungs of rats. Instead of using talcum powder, dust your feet (and other parts of the body) with cornstarch to absorb moisture.

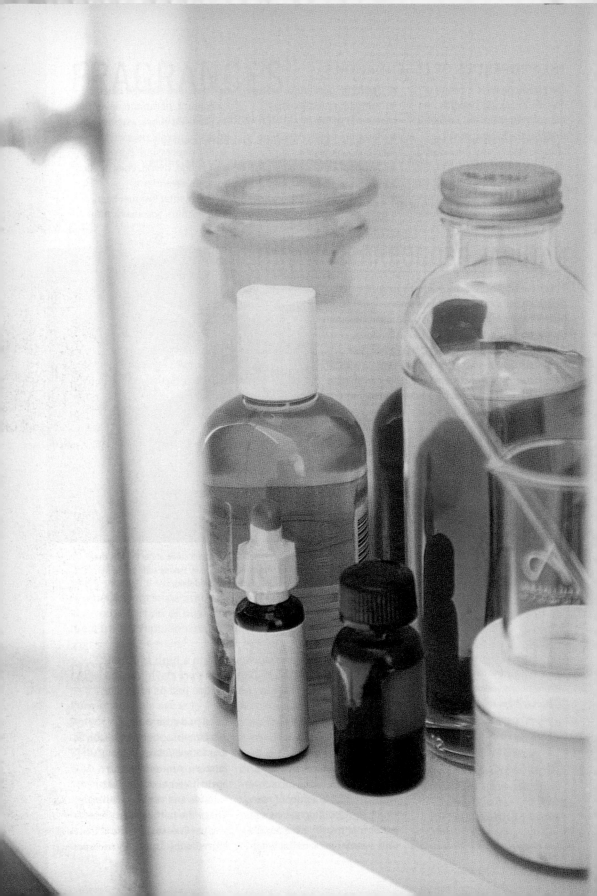

NATURAL REMEDIES

Hangover cure p128

For common ailments, it is not always necessary to pay a visit to the doctor or to buy over-the-counter remedies at the pharmacy. There are many natural cures and complementary therapies that avoid the use of drugs and leave you free of side effects. Homeopathy is a valuable "alternative" medicine that bases treatment on an analysis of your personal profile. Acupuncture has been proven to relieve many ailments, herbalism is a powerful form of medicine, and aromatherapy and massage treat a number of complaints successfully. Osteopaths and chiropractors are now endorsed by conventional medical practitioners, and the Alexander Technique has helped many people with back and neck problems, among other complaints. To find recommended practitioners in complementary therapies, see Resources page 172.

Garlic antiseptic p129

STAYING HEALTHY

You can do a great deal to prevent problems from arising in the first place by taking up various forms of bodywork: yoga, Pilates, and T'ai Chi all offer positive health benefits. Yoga is renowned for its relaxing and balancing effects, as well as for toning the body, and it also strengthens the immune system. Pilates keeps the skeletal-muscular system strong, and T'ai Chi maintains a balance of physical and mental fitness. To ease anxiety and depression, and to relieve stress, meditation has been proved to be an effective aid.

Chamomile tea p130

Keep a range of natural remedies in your bathroom cabinet to deal with minor ailments that can be treated safely at home.

Simple meditation p133

COMMON AILMENTS

A surprising range of everyday ailments can be treated successfully with food plants such as onions (antibiotic), garlic (antiseptic and antibiotic), and lemon (antioxidant). Many cooking ingredients, such as vinegar, baking soda, salt, honey, and oats, also form the basis of natural remedies. Herbs such as thyme (antiseptic and antifungal) and lavender (a carminative and an antidepressant), and spices such as cloves (antibacterial) and ginger (antispasmodic) offer safe, cheap, and easy-to-use remedies. Remember also that water is one of nature's greatest healers: when you are unwell, always drink plenty of filtered water to flush the toxins out of your system.

THE NATURAL MEDICINE CHEST

Common ailments – from colds and sore throats to insect bites – can all be treated successfully without recourse to medicinal drugs. With just a handful of everyday ingredients, you will have the basis for a natural medicine chest and first aid kit.

COUGHS & COLDS

● To soothe a chesty cough, place 1 teaspoon of chopped root ginger (an antispasmodic), 1–2 tablespoons of honey, and a squeeze of lemon juice in a mug of boiling water, and drink 3–4 times a day.

● A cup of hot water containing 2 teaspoons of cider vinegar makes a good decongestant for a cough.

● For a cold, finely chop a few cloves of garlic (or the same amount of raw onion), cover with honey and leave for 2–3 hours, then take teaspoonfuls throughout the day.

● Echinacea is an excellent remedy for a cold, plus soluble vitamin C (up to 500mg per day).

CHILBLAINS

● Mix 1 teaspoon of cayenne or chilli powder with 1 tablespoon of base oil (*see page 124*) and rub into the affected area; this improves the circulation and relieves inflammation.

EARACHE

● Warm a little olive oil. Prick a garlic clove with a pin and leave to soak in the oil for a few minutes. Pour a little of the infused oil into the ear and plug with cotton wool.

For a hangover, blend together banana, soya milk, and fruit concentrate. Drink this mixture to help line the stomach and absorb toxins produced by alcohol consumption.

For headaches, soak a cotton wool pad in 200ml (7fl oz) water and 1 teaspoon of dried mint, and place over the eyes.

HANGOVERS

● Blend 3 small red chillies with 600ml (1 pint) tomato juice and a dash of soy sauce. Drink as much as you can. This releases endorphins – natural painkillers – into the body.
● Blend 1 peeled banana with 600ml (1 pint) soya milk and 2 tablespoons of fruit juice of your choice. Chill the mixture, and drink.
● Eat two apples first thing in the morning. This will help to replace lost vitamins and reduce the effects of dehydration.

HOMEMADE GINGER ALE FOR NAUSEA

Grate about 175g (6oz) fresh ginger root, place it in a pan with 450ml (15fl oz) water, and bring to the boil. Simmer for 5 minutes, then leave to stand for 24 hours. Strain through muslin, return the juice to a pan and add 300ml (10fl oz) honey. Simmer for 5 minutes, then cool and bottle. Store in the fridge. Take 1 tablespoon of the mixture in a glass of soda water as required.

HEADACHES

● Make a ginger poultice to relieve head tension. Mix 2 tablespoons of ground ginger with a little water and warm gently in a saucepan. Spread onto a lint pad and press on to the forehead. Lie down in a quiet, dark room while you allow the treatment to work.
● Drink a tea made from 1 teaspoon each of chopped lemon grass, fennel seeds, and cardamom. Lie down with a scarf over your eyes and rest.
● Peppermint, rosemary, or sage teas are all helpful in relieving headaches.

INSECT BITES & STINGS

● Mix 1 teaspoon of baking soda and a little water or vinegar into a paste, and apply directly to the sting.
● Rub a few drops of neat lavender essential oil directly on to the affected area.
● Rub the cut side of an onion on to a wasp or bee sting.
● Catnip has been found to be an effective insect – and especially mosquito – repellent: rub fresh leaves over exposed skin, or buy extract of catnip.

SORE THROAT

● A simple mixture of hot fresh lemon juice sweetened with honey is one of the oldest and best remedies for a sore throat.
● Make a salt water solution with 2 tablespoons of salt and 300ml (½ pint) warm water. Use as a gargle.
● Heat 1 tablespoon each of honey and brown sugar with 3 tablespoons cider vinegar. Add a clove of garlic and leave to infuse. Cool, and use as a gargle to soothe a sore throat.

STOMACH PROBLEMS

● Soda bicarbonate acts as a gentle antacid in cases of indigestion or heartburn. Mix 2 teaspoons of soda bicarbonate with 50ml (2fl oz) of water; stir.
● Drink fresh lemon or lime juice mixed with a little water for stomachache.
● Ginger has a soothing effect on the digestive system and is useful for travel sickness and early morning sickness in pregnancy: drink ginger tea or chew a little piece of the root.
● A cup of black tea goes a long way to soothing an upset stomach.

A peeled garlic clove rubbed directly on to a cut will prevent infection.

SMALL WOUNDS & CUTS

● Garlic is antiseptic, and onion antibacterial: apply either to a small cut to keep it clean and germ-free.
● Lavender essential oil can be applied neat to burns or cuts. It helps heals them quickly, preventing scarring.

THE HERBAL MEDICINE CHEST

There are plenty of natural remedies based on plants and herbs that are available to treat and cure most of the minor complaints that affect us. Like conventional drugs, these are produced commercially, but they do not contain added synthetic chemicals. If your home medicine cabinet is filled with over-the-counter drugs and medications, it is worth knowing that many manufactured drugs contain artificial colourings and flavourings, preservatives, alcohol, and sugars. Antacids, for example, which are used to treat symptoms of heartburn and indigestion, may contain aluminium compounds, which have been associated with the onset of Alzheimer's disease – so replace these synthetic remedies with the herbal ones described below.

Treat insomnia or indigestion with a soothing cup of fresh chamomile tea.

USING HERBS SAFELY

Herbal remedies may come from natural sources, and have fewer, if any, of the side effects of conventional drugs. They should still be treated with care, however, since high concentrations of plant substances can be as toxic as ordinary medicines.

- Read the directions for use carefully and never exceed the stated dose.
- Do not take more than two internal herbal remedies at the same time, or one internal and one external.
- If symptoms persist, consult a professional practitioner.

- Never give infants under six months internal medicines without professional advice.
- During the first three months of pregnancy all medicines – herbal included – should be avoided completely, including essential oils. Get professional advice if you wish to use herbs or essential oils after the first trimester.
- Never take essential oils internally, and dilute for external use except where specified.
- If you are on medication, ask your doctor if it is safe to take a herbal remedy.

HERBS DURING PREGNANCY

Most culinary herbs are safe to eat during pregnancy. The following herbs are important exceptions, however. You must avoid them at all costs, either in food or medicinally, since they can stimulate the muscles of the uterus and result in a miscarriage.

- Blue cohosh (*Caulophyllum thalictroides*)
- Goldenseal (*Hydrastis canadensis*)
- Juniper (*Juniperus communis*)
- Pennyroyal (*Mentha pulegium*)
- Sage (*Salvia officinalis*)
- Yarrow (*Achillea millefolium*)

> **WARNING**
> The following nine essential oils are not recommended for external use during pregnancy: basil, chamomile, juniper, lavender, marjoram, myrrh, pennyroyal, sage, and thyme.

NATURAL REMEDIES TO STOCK

The herbal remedies listed here should be available from most health food stores and some chemists. Always read the instructions on the packaging, and take particular note of any cautions. Always check with a doctor before taking a herbal remedy if you have any serious medical condition.

PREPARATION	USE
ALOE VERA	
Cream	Minor burns and scalds, sunburn, stretch marks, warts, wounds and grazes, eczema
Lotion	Use as gently soothing, astringent skin cream
ARNICA	
Cream	Bruises, sprains, aching muscles
Homeopathic tablets	Emotional shock, injury, pain, and trauma
CALENDULA	
Cream	Acne, boils, athlete's foot, bites and stings, nappy rash, bruises, minor wounds, and swellings
CHAMOMILE	
Oil	Nappy rash: 3 drops German chamomile in 6 tsp almond oil
Cream	Sore and itchy skin, bites and stings, sore nipples, eczema, and muscle spasms
Tea	Insomnia, indigestion, morning sickness, baby colic (use German chamomile)
CLOVE	
Essential oil	For toothache: 1–2 drops on cotton wool, dabbed on to sore area
COMFREY	
Ointment	Bruises, acne, boils, fractures and wounds, fungal skin infections, psoriasis, stiff and aching joints
ECHINACEA	
Tablets or tincture	Stimulates immune system when under attack, for use in colds, flu, coughs, and fevers. Also mild asthma, and cold sores
GARLIC	
Capsules	Increases resistance to infection: use for colds and flu, coughs, and bronchitis. Helps to lower blood pressure. Use for cold sores, and digestive infections
HYPERICUM	
Cream	Cramp, neuralgia, cold sores, back pain, stiff and aching joints and muscles
Oil	Minor wounds and burns

PREPARATION	USE
LAVENDER	
Essential oil	For back pain, irritability, asthma, headaches: 5–6 drops in 20ml (4 tsp) base oil. For insect stings and bites, use undiluted. For insomnia, stiff and aching joints: 8–10 drops in bath water
MEADOWSWEET	
Tea	Stomach acidity, heartburn, and diarrhoea
Tablets	Rheumatic aches
NEEM	
Oil	Head lice, skin rashes, ringworm. Also a powerful insect repellent.
Cream	Eczema, psoriasis, and acne
SLIPPERY ELM	
Capsules	Coughs, bronchitis
Powder	Acidity, indigestion
Tablets	Diarrhoea, irritable bowel syndrome, haemorrhoids
TEA TREE	
Essential oil	For stings, burns, wounds, skin infection, ringworm, athlete's foot, warts and corns, acne and boils: 4–5 drops per 15ml (3 tsp) base oil. For vaginal thrush: 2–3 drops oil in 1 tsp olive oil on a tampon, insert for 2–3 hours at a time; and 8–10 drops in bath water with a cup of cider vinegar
THYME	
Essential oil	For scabies, bites and stings, sciatica and rheumatic pains, ringworm, athlete's foot, and thrush: 3–4 drops in 1 tsp base oil
VALERIAN & HOPS	
Tablets	Insomnia; calming in times of stress, tension, and anxiety
WHITE WILLOW	
Tablets	Arthritis, rheumatic pain, back pain, stiff knees and hips, high fevers. Also reduces night sweats and hot flushes in menopause
WITCH HAZEL	
Distilled	Insect stings, sore skin, rashes, broken and varicose veins, bruises, and eczema

HEALING THROUGH BODYWORK

Taking up the practices of yoga and meditation can do much to prevent as well as to cure minor body ailments, while improving your quality of life at the same time. Yoga leads to a better balance of body, mind, and spirit, and the stillness of meditation brings calm, clarity, and a sense of perspective to life issues. Neither practice is difficult: anyone is capable, at any age, and in any condition. Also, yoga and meditation exercises do not have to be particularly demanding: doing just a little on a regular basis will make a difference to your general level of fitness and your sense of well-being. Invest in comfortable, loose-fitting clothes in natural fabrics for your yoga practice and aim to allocate a time in your day so that yoga becomes a habit. Establish a routine so that practising becomes a part of your everyday life: the benefits are huge.

If you have been practising yoga for a while and are quite supple, perform this long back stretch to increase neck and spine flexibility and open up the chest.

YOGA

Yoga is a philosophy that originated in northern India around 5,000 years ago. The combination of physical work, mental focus, and breathing exercises has an impact on many aspects of your being, although yoga as now practised in the West concentrates mainly on the physical element. Through a series of exercises, known as asanas, yoga increases strength and stamina, suppleness and flexibility, improves posture and concentration, reduces stress, brings deep relaxation, and promotes a sense of well-being and balance. The asanas should be practised in coordination with the in- and out-breath. Find a teacher to help you adopt the correct postures, and invest in a good yoga book (*see Resources page 177*).

This simple side stretch will improve your balance and increase the strength in your arms and legs, as well as stretching and toning your waist. Hold for a few minutes, then repeat the same stretch on the left side of your body.

GUIDELINES FOR YOGA PRACTICE

- Practise in a quiet, warm room away from distractions such as the telephone.
- Wear loose clothing so that you can stretch, and perform the exercises in bare feet.
- Always allow three hours to elapse after eating a full meal, or two hours after a light one, before practising yoga.
- If you have any specific medical problems, inform a qualified yoga teacher – there may be specific asanas that will benefit your medical problem (or ones to avoid).
- Do not attempt advanced postures such as the headstand until you are practised at yoga: you could damage your back and neck muscles and joints.
- Remember that yoga is not a competition, so work at your own pace and level of flexibility.

MEDITATION

Practices of meditation derive from many cultures, and there are numerous techniques. Whichever method you choose, the aim is to heighten your awareness of the present moment and to leave you with a calm, expansive mind and a feeling of peace. Research has shown that mediation can help relieve stress, high blood pressure, cardiac disease, chronic pain, psoriasis, and even some cancers, including breast and prostate cancer. Immune function improves too, so a regular practice of "sitting" can be not only enjoyable but also improve your health.

To put it simply, meditation may be defined as "stopping and breathing". Stopping means stopping the mind from engaging with its chattering thoughts (the ancient Indian texts call it the "monkey-mind"), so for most of us that means stilling the body too.

You can meditate on the train, or for a few moments at work. However, for most people the way to start is to find a quiet place to sit, perhaps with a candle and an incense stick, in a clean, warm, and uncluttered room. You can sit cross-legged on the floor, or kneel unaided or with the help of a kneeling stool. If this is uncomfortable, sit on an upright chair with your back supported. In both cases, keep your spine upright but relaxed, your hands resting in your lap, and your face relaxed. You can close your eyes or keep them open.

A SIMPLE MEDITATION

- Sit comfortably on the floor or a chair.
- Make sure your shoulders, neck, and jaw are relaxed, and your body soft.
- Become aware of your breathing, noticing the rise and fall of the abdomen on each inhalation and exhalation.
- Keep your attention focused on the breath: if it strays, say to yourself "breathing in" as you inhale and "breathing out" as you exhale, to help focus the mind.
- Build up this practice from 5 minutes or so until you can easily maintain it for 20 minutes. As with any skill, it's a question of practice, of acquiring a kind of "fitness" for mental focus, and of learning the habit of quietness.

Sit still with your palms in your lap, your back straight, and your body relaxed, and concentrate on your breathing.

BABY CARE

It is natural for parents to want to provide the best possible start in life for a new baby. Infants are especially susceptible to pollutants in the environment and often react negatively to synthetic chemicals: in the past decade there has been a doubling of asthmatic conditions in children under five, and an increase in allergies in children. In the home, children may be exposed to hormone-disrupters in certain types of plastics, pesticides and fertilizers in food, tobacco smoke, cadmium and other heavy metals in house dust, untested chemicals in toiletries, and paints and other household furnishing fibres that "off-gas" chemical fumes. Keeping the home free of as many of these substances as possible, and making sure that it is clean, will go a long way to ensuring the health and safety of babies and young children.

ORGANICS FOR CHILDREN

We can make a substantial contribution to counteracting the negative impact of such household pollutants. Follow the advice offered in this chapter and feed your children on wholesome home cooking made from organic ingredients, avoid plastics by selecting natural furnishing and bedding materials such as wood, wool, cotton, leather, and metal, and dress them in clothes made from 100 per cent natural fibres. Decorate their nursery or bedroom with non-toxic paints and finishes, and so provide them with a room that is free of synthetics and chemicals and has a greatly improved air quality. You may not find all these child-friendly products in the average high street store just yet, but there is plenty available by ordering through the internet or by mail order.

Natural fibres such as organic wool and cotton will provide your baby with an allergy-free, non-toxic start in life.

Healthy baby food p136

Nappy choices p138

Organic bedding p140

Cleaning toys p141

NAPPIES & SKIN CARE

A baby's skin is soft, thin, and delicate and must be treated with the utmost care. It can more readily absorb chemicals which may be present in various products, ranging from disposable nappies to baby creams and skin lotions. In addition, the environmental impact of plastic disposable nappies is considerable, not only in their manufacture, but also as a major contributor to household waste, and thus to air and water pollution.

CHOOSING & USING NAPPIES

Reusable nappies are available in organic cotton. Some have integral tying string, so don't need pins. Nappy liners can also be used, plus woollen nappy covers, which will keep your baby warm in cold weather and cool when it is hot.

As a baby, your child will use about 5,000 nappies, and approximately 4 per cent of all household waste consists of soiled nappies. The pros and cons of disposable versus cloth nappies are outlined below.

CLOTH NAPPIES

● Cloth nappies are much more absorbent than their disposable equivalents.
● Folded cloth nappies are awkward to use, but fitted versions are now available.
● Although the initial cost of buying cloth nappies is higher, in the long run it comes to less than half of what you pay out on disposables, even after taking laundering into account.
● Cloth nappies can be used for subsequent babies, or can be recycled.
● Washing cloth nappies is far better for the environment than throwing away several non-biodegradable disposables on a daily basis. Local nappy services are now in operation in most cities (*see Resources page 172*) and will launder nappies for you. These services use 32 per cent less energy than home washing, and 41 per cent less water because of their bulk loads and commercial machines.

DISPOSABLES

● Disposable nappies are made from synthetic fibres that contain deodorizing chemicals, bleaches, and highly toxic dioxins that are all harmful to the environment. These cause skin rashes on sensitive baby skin – nappy rash was practically unknown before 1950 when disposable nappies were introduced.
● Worldwide, literally millions of disposables are used per day, and end up in landfill sites where they remain for years – they may take 10 years or more to decompose.
● Millions of trees per year are cut down to produce just the absorbent paper "fluff" in disposable nappies.

To soak cloth nappies, you will need a bucket with a lid. Half fill the bucket with cold water and stir in 3–4 tablespoons of borax or baking soda, to deodorize and reduce staining.

USING CLOTH NAPPIES

- Use 100 per cent organic cotton nappies.
- Buy enough to allow for laundering and drying: three dozen should be adequate.
- Invest in washable gauze nappy liners that make cleaning easier, rather than disposable paper ones.
- Buy at least two buckets with lids, a supply of borax and/or baking soda, and "soft chemistry" washing powder for pre-soaking soiled nappies before laundering.
- Let your baby go without nappies as often as possible to expose its skin to the fresh air.
- Do not feel guilty about using the occasional disposable when convenient.

CLEANING CLOTH NAPPIES

Rinse wet nappies and dispose of solid matter down the toilet. Place the nappies in a bucket with a borax or baking soda solution, and leave to soak for 6–8 hours or overnight. Drain the soaking solution down the toilet. Machine-wash the nappies on a hot cycle at 21°C (70°F), with a double rinse. Dry outside if possible: sunshine is a natural bleach and disinfectant. If you have to tumble-dry, it will help to sterilize the nappies.

BABY SKIN CARE

Because baby skin is so delicate and sensitive, avoid using strong soaps and shampoos made for adults on your baby. Additives such as artificial colours, fragrances, and preservatives can cause irritation and allergic reactions. Choose plant-based, natural, organic oils and creams (*see Resources page 172*). These products are not tested on animals, are biodegradable, and can be guaranteed to be free of synthetics and petrochemicals.

- Never use soap products on a baby's face – the skin here is more sensitive than elsewhere.
- Use lotions, oils, and powders that come from natural and organic sources, such as almond oil and cocoa butter.
- Dry your baby with a soft cotton towel and avoid talcum powder. Accidental inhalation of talc has been linked to serious illness and even death.

- Buy nappy cream containing ingredients such as red clover, a natural anti-inflammatory.
- Use shampoo containing chamomile oil, which is gentle for baby hair.
- Treat skin rashes with calendula cream.
- For nappy rash, mix 3 drops of German chamomile oil with 30ml (6 teaspoons) of almond oil and rub on the affected area.

Chemical-free baby toiletries, including baby toothpaste, are now available from organic supermarkets and health shops.

CLOTHES, BEDDING, & TOYS

The chances are that your new baby will move into a newly decorated room. If it is your first child, it may have a new cot, mattress, and bedding. Be aware that new paint, carpet, vinyl wallpaper, synthetic mattresses, and non-iron sheets may all "off-gas" chemical fumes. To give your new baby the best start in life, keep these toxins to a minimum by choosing natural fibres and decorating products where possible. If your local shops do not supply what you want, there are plenty of mail-order outlets that do (*see Resources page 172*).

BABY CLOTHES

Babies grow so fast that their clothes never get much wear, and so remain in good condition. Why not save a small fortune by exchanging with friends, or buying second-hand in charity shops or through local newspaper advertisements?

● When buying clothing new, avoid synthetic fibres and formaldehyde finishes.
● Make sure that sleepwear is not treated with flameproof chemicals that your baby will inhale during sleep. Buy natural fabrics instead – wool, cotton, linen, and hemp (*see Resources page 172*). These are less flammable than synthetics and so will minimize any fire hazards to which babies and young children might be exposed.
● If possible, buy clothes made from natural fibres that have been organically produced, and so contain no chemical residues.

BEDDING

Fibres that "breathe" will help your child rest more comfortably and reduce exposure to toxins during sleep. Opening the bedroom window to let in plenty of fresh air is also beneficial.

● Choose a mattress carefully. Most mattresses, whether for adults or for babies, are filled with polyurethane foam, covered with polyester, and treated with flameproof chemicals. In addition,

Organic cotton baby clothes, towels, and bed sets are free of synthetic chemical finishes or treatments.

many cot mattresses have an extra plastic covering for waterproofing. Babies spend many more hours in their beds asleep than adults, and have no choice but to inhale the gases emitted by these substances for protracted periods. You are unlikely to find what you want in high-street stores, so try mail order companies that sell mattresses with natural and even organic coverings and fillings in cotton or wool (*see Resources page 172*).

● Bed sheets and covers are also available in natural and organic fibres, and are no more labour-intensive than synthetic bedlinen with non-iron finishes. Cotton sheets and pillow slips do not need ironing if the washing instructions are followed correctly, and they are hung out to dry outside, then smoothed flat before folding.

● Buy your baby a wooden cot made from sustainable wood (*see Resources page 172*).

TOYS

The prevalence of plastic in children's toys is overwhelming. It may seem that there is no choice but to surround your children with playthings that "off-gas" and turn the nursery into a toxic zone. Many children's toys are made from PVC – polyvinyl chloride – otherwise known as vinyl, whose manufacture and disposal creates dioxins, highly toxic substances. Soft vinyl toys may contain phthalates, which are banned in some European countries. These chemicals may leak from the toy when sucked, chewed, squeezed, or even just held. The European Science Committee has advised that phthalates are liable to cause liver, kidney, and testicular damage and may affect hormones and lead to reduced fertility in later life.

● Plastic toys are non-biodegradable and eventually increase the amount of plastic in landfill sites.

● To avoid plastics, give your babies and children toys made from natural materials such as wood, cotton, wool, fleece, paper, leather, and metal.

● Toys made from natural materials tend to last longer and can be recycled by donating them to charity or to friends with children.

● Join the local toy library and borrow toys and books: this gives your child more variety and saves money.

● Make your own playthings with your children from simple everyday objects (little boxes, jars, desk supplies, toilet rolls), as well as natural objects such as seashells and pine cones, and stock up with natural paints to decorate them with.

● Save your old clothes for a dressing-up box.

● Save paper for your children and their friends to draw on, and magazines for them to cut up for making collages.

CLEANING TOYS

● To clean soiled plastic or wooden toys, dissolve 2 heaped tablespoons of baking soda in 600ml (1 pint) warm water. Either submerge the toy and soak it, or wipe it clean, then rinse in cold water and leave to dry naturally.

● To clean a fluffy toy, place in a large plastic bag with some baking soda, seal the bag and shake vigorously from time to time over a period of several hours. Brush the baking soda out of the fur with a stiff brush, and the toy will look like new.

A dusting of baking soda eliminates odours and removes unwanted stains from soiled soft toys.

KEEPING PETS

Pets provide great affection and companionship, but animals kept in the home will also raise greater health and hygiene issues than, say, ducks, and geese, which are kept outside. In this chapter, the focus is on caring for dogs and cats, because they are the animals that the majority of people wish to keep in their home. There are guidelines on how to maintain a clean, allergy-free environment without resorting to strong chemicals. Advice is also given on how to prevent unwanted hair loss by regular grooming, and to remove fluff from carpets and soft furnishings, together with ways pet owners can maintain high standards of hygiene by keeping pets off beds and furniture.

PEST CONTROL

During the warmer summer months, pests such as fleas and ticks are picked up on the coats of animals. Rather than relying on chemical flea treatments, pests can be controlled naturally using simple recipes based on essential oils. Pet urine and excreta can also be a problem in the home, especially with young animals. Contact with excreta is especially harmful to children, so it must be cleaned up safely in the home, garden, and public places. The odours and stains resulting from urine and excreta can be treated naturally, too.

RESPONSIBLE BUYS

Before buying a pet, bear in mind that there are thousands of animals in rescue centres that need homes. If you are choosing a bird, reptile, or tropical fish, make sure that it has been bred in captivity and has not been taken from the wild (*see Resources page 173*).

A small, wire-haired dog like this border terrier needs regular grooming to prevent it from shedding unwanted hairs in the home.

Pet foods p145

Vitamin supplements p145

Healthy coat p147

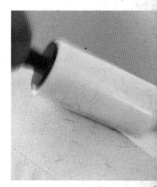

Removing pet hairs p150

FEEDING YOUR PET

Many of the pet foods on the market make great claims to be "complete", but do not take into account that dogs, and to some extent cats, benefit from plant nutrients. Before domestication, these plant nutrients would have been available in the wild when eating the entrails of prey that had grazed on pasture. Commercial pet foods lack this natural diversity and compensate by introducing chemical additives, which are thought by some vets to trigger allergies and weaken the immune system.

Keep leftover vegetables to feed to your dog as a healthy addition to its diet.

Holistic vets recognize that the best diet for dogs and cats is principally raw organic meat, plus some vegetable scraps and minimal supplements. Pets on this varied diet have fewer digestive problems, and are less susceptible to parasites, skin ailments, and a build-up of tartar on teeth.

PET FOOD FACTS

Although convenient for pet owners, tinned or dried animal foods may not necessarily be good for your pet or the environment. The following facts will help you to make an informed decision about the foods available and help you to decide for yourself.

- Pet foods contain a wide range of chemicals. These include pesticides, nitrates, lead, synthetic preservatives, and artificial flavourings and colourings.
- All pet foods are made up from livestock carcasses, and are high in animal fats.

- They contain salt and high levels of sugar to make them more palatable.
- About three-quarters of the contents of canned pet food is water.
- Canned pet foods may contain lead from the soldering of the cans (see page 79).

- Dry cat foods have been linked to kidney problems in cats on this diet, especially if they don't drink enough water. A balanced diet of different types of food is best for the health of your cat. If your cat has a bladder disorder, you may want to avoid dry cat food.

DIETARY IMPROVEMENTS

The following dietary programme works very well for my pets. However, not all vets would support such a feeding programme. Always consult either your own vet or a holistic vet before following a homemade diet for your pet.

- Feed your dog one-third raw meat or fish to two-thirds vegetables and cereals.
- Cooked brown rice is very nutritious, as are nuts and seeds and all vegetables.
- For cats, create a diet consisting of three-quarters raw meat or fish, topped up by

vegetables, cooked grains, and raw oats soaked in milk. This should result in a calmer nature, improved resistance to infection, and fewer flea and parasite infestations.
- Make friends with your local butcher. Ask for kidney, liver, heart, and tripe.

● Fish is an excellent protein for dogs and cats, and the essential fatty acids Omega-3 and Omega-6 in fish will boost your pet's immune system.

● To save money, buy meat bones in bulk and freeze them.

● Dilute cats' milk with water.

● Do not give cats cream: it is too rich for them and gives them indigestion.

● Let cats and dogs graze on herbs and grasses. Parsley is a digestive tonic, dandelion a liver-toner, and goosegrass cleanses the lymphatic system.

Let your pet enjoy a varied diet that includes raw meat and vegetables as an alternative to tinned and dried foods.

VITAMIN SUPPLEMENTS

The following supplements help treat a host of pet complaints and are suitable for both cats and dogs. Add the capsules to your pet's food to make pill-taking more palatable.

Available from good pet stores and veterinary practices, vitamin supplements should be taken as directed.

BREWERS' YEAST

This soothes nerves in animals as it does in humans, and also works as a flea-deterrent. Give 25mg per 5kg (11lb) bodyweight.

COD LIVER OIL

This eases stiff joints and skin problems in both humans and animals. Give 1 capsule or teaspoon per day.

GARLIC CAPSULES

To deter parasites and act as a natural antiseptic, give 1 garlic capsule or clove in food daily.

SEAWEED

This supplement has benefits for cats and dogs including: a shinier coat; improved alertness; healthier teeth and gums, and better bowel function. Give according to packet instructions.

SUNFLOWER OIL

To prevent dry, flaky skin, add 1 teaspoon of sunflower oil to your pet's food each day.

WHEATGERM OIL

This calms skin complaints, the nervous system, and encourages healthy reproduction. Give your pet 2 teaspoons per day, in food.

PEST CONTROL

The pesticides used in animal pest-control products are strong chemicals, leaving dogs, cats, and small mammals exposed to toxins. Impregnated flea collars can cause contact dermatitis, and may give off chemical fumes that you, your children, and your pet inhale. You and your family will also come into contact with the chemicals in pet flea sprays and shampoos, among which may be organophosphate and carbamate compounds, with active ingredients such as the nerve poisons propoxur (very toxic orally), diazinon (linked to dozens of pet deaths and also toxic to bees), and carbaryl (a potential human carcinogen). The pesticides amitraz and permethrin are suspected endocrine disrupters. Pets treated with these chemicals may have symptoms such as vomiting, depression, lethargy, diarrhoea, loss of appetite, and itchy skin.

FLEAS

Although we are encouraged to believe by pharmaceutical companies that strong chemical sprays are the only hygienic way to prevent or rid domestic animals of a flea infestation, there are many natural alternatives that were in common usage before the introduction of chemical products. The following tips explain how to control pests the natural way to keep your home free of toxins.

HOMEMADE CAT FLEA COLLAR

This simple recipe uses a blend of hydrosols or hydrolats, also known as herbal waters (see Resources page 173), to make a fragrant cat collar that repels fleas. I make one for my cat every summer and it is very effective. Use hydrosols rather than essential oils for cats because they metabolize them more effectively. When you have mixed the alcohol, hydrosols, and garlic oil together in a small bowl, soak the felt collar in the liquid until it has absorbed it all. Allow the collar to dry, then put it around your pet's neck. The flea-repellent effect will last for about four weeks before you need to treat the collar again.

YOU WILL NEED
Soft felt cat collar
2 teaspoons pure alcohol (vodka will do)
1 tablespoon rosemary hydrosol
1 tablespoon lemon verbena hydrosol
1 tablespoon lavender hydrosol
1 tablespoon pennyroyal hydrosol
oil squeezed from 4 garlic capsules

A felt cat collar soaked in herbal hydrosols and garlic is repellent to fleas and will keep your cat free of infestations.

OTHER NATURAL FLEA DETERRENTS

- Pet flea combs are available from most pet shops. They are fine-toothed so that they can trap adult fleas, but they also pick out the dried blood and flea faeces in pet fur on which the larvae feed. After combing, dunk any fleas that are caught on the comb into warm soapy water to kill them. Flush the used soapy water down the toilet to avoid further infestation.
- When bathing pets, make a rinse out of pennyroyal or wormwood herb tea (do not use these herbs on pregnant pets). Make the infusion strong and allow it to cool before use.
- Pennyroyal or wormwood powder is also available from some vets; they are not recommended for pregnant pets. Sprinkle the powder on to your pet's coat and then rub it in vigorously. Leave for 10–15 minutes before bathing the animal.
- Add brewers' yeast powder or capsules – approximately 25mg per 5kg (11lb) bodyweight – to your pet's food daily during an infestation to deter fleas.
- Add 1 garlic capsule to your pet's food each day to deter fleas and prevent roundworm.
- Add 1 teaspoon of cider vinegar to your pet's drinking water on a daily basis.
- Make up a blend of 5 drops of tea tree oil to 1 eggcupful of sunflower oil, and massage this into your dog's coat: it is antiseptic, soothes itchy skins, and deters fleas.
- To remove fleas from pet bedding, wash it regularly.
- Regular vacuuming, especially of pets' sleeping areas, sucks up flea eggs and helps to prevent re-infestation.
- Try using an electric flea trap as an alternative to chemical sprays. This works by emitting gentle heat that attracts fleas and traps them on sticky paper.
- Pet rabbits and guinea pigs can be treated with the natural insecticide spray Xenex.

TICKS

If your pet picks up a tick, do not attempt to pull it out of your animal's coat: half of it will be left in the skin and can cause infection. Carefully hold the end of a lit cigarette to the tick to make it release its hold.

HOMEMADE DOG FLEA MASSAGE OIL

This is the mixture I use on my dog at the height of the summer flea infestation: increase or double the quantities for larger dogs. Omit the pennyroyal oil if your dog is pregnant.

YOU WILL NEED

1 eggcupful of sunflower oil
3 drops orange oil
3 drops citronella oil
3 drops lemon oil
3 drops tea tree oil
1 drop pennyroyal oil (use with extreme caution as in high doses it can be extremely toxic)

Mix together the sunflower oil and essential oils in a glass bowl and gently massage the mixture into your dog's coat, using your fingertips. Your pet should enjoy the massage and the attention, and will smell wonderful. Perform this treatment every other day until the fleas subside.

1 Mix together the essential oils in a small glass dish, taking care to add no more than 1 drop of pennyroyal oil.

2 Add the sunflower oil to act as a base for the essential oils. Massage the blend into your dog's fur.

PET HEALTH

Part of the responsibility of keeping pets is to make sure that they are healthy. They need regular check-ups and a programme of vaccinations to boost their immune systems. Vet bills can be expensive, so find a reputable pet insurance scheme that offers comprehensive cover. However, some people believe that pets do not need to be vaccinated as often as the drug companies recommend. Trials show that only a small percentage of animals vaccinated are really protected against fatal diseases, and that hygiene and nutrition have contributed as much to disease control as vaccination programmes. Also, as with humans, vaccines may cause side effects in pets.

Homeopathic treatment and alternative medicine is also available for pets: it has a good record for behavioural, emotional and stress problems, travel sickness, nasal problems, colitis, allergies, long-term diarrhoea, and arthritis. Chronic skin problems, and eye and ear infections are better remedied with drugs. If you have several pets, keep a natural first aid kit at home to treat your animals for minor complaints – not only will this avoid trips to the vet, which can be stressful for pets, but it will also save on vet's bills.

FIRST AID

Like human homeopathic remedies, those for pets are based on natural plant, animal, and mineral substances and are entirely free of chemicals. If possible, keep a medicine box of the following homeopathic remedies. Store them in a cool, dry place out of direct sunlight. To treat your pet, use the pipette to place 2–3 drops of the remedy in the animal's mouth. Try not to allow the pipette to touch the animal and contaminate the remedy. In acute cases, dose your pet every 20–30 minutes, in less acute cases, every 1–2 hours, and in chronic conditions 2–3 times a day.

- Arnica: shock, bruising or swelling; for soothing before and after an operation or birth trauma; for eye injuries.
- Aconite: shock, trauma (after a road accident, for example); for fights with other animals, during thunderstorms or fireworks; for difficult birthing, haemorrhage; fever if thirsty and restless; sunburn if onset is acute and animal is restless.
- Apis: bee or wasp stings.
- Arsenicum: acute diarrhoea or vomiting.

- Belladonna: temperature, fever, and inflammation.
- Hypericum: animal bites.
- Heparsulph: infected wounds, burst abscesses, and wound pain.
- Rhus tox: arthritis, joint sprains, and stiffness in the mornings; for working dogs before and after going out.
- Sulphur: itchy skin (you can also buy small blocks of solid sulphur to place in your pet's water bowl, where they will leach into the water. These blocks of sulphur are available from good pet shops).
- Symphytum: to promote healing of broken bones.

TOP TIP

To give your dog medicine, grasp its upper jaw with one hand to prevent biting. Hold the pipette in your free hand and place the liquid at the back of the dog's tongue.

ALLERGIES

Like humans, domestic animals can suffer acute allergic reactions to chemicals and solvents such as formaldehyde that are used in carpet production. Many pets are also adversely affected by air-fresheners and other chemical cleaning sprays.

● Avoid proprietary brands of pet shampoos: they are likely to contain strong chemicals that cause allergies. Use organic pet shampoos instead.
● Avoid spray-on or dust-on carpet cleaners, which may cause severe skin problems on contact with your pet's belly.
● Using "soft chemistry" floor cleaners and bleaches will reduce the amount of toxic chemicals that your pet is likely to come into contact with.
● When re-carpeting or putting down a new floor, choose natural, untreated materials (*see pages 42–43*).
● Use natural air fresheners in your home (*see page 49*).

COAT & SKIN CARE

Keeping your dog or cat well-groomed will remove dead skin cells and dirt from the fur and prevent skin problems from developing. Long-haired pets will need daily grooming and short-haired types weekly brushing to keep in condition.

GROOMING YOUR PET

● If you have the outdoor space, groom your pet outside to prevent hairs, skin particles, and dirt from being released into your home environment.
● During times of year when flea infestation is at its height, groom daily with a flea-comb if possible (*see page 147*).
● To ensure complete removal of fleas and mites, wash your pet's brush and comb immediately after grooming, and leave them in a warm place to dry.

1 Calm your dog and encourage it to sit or stand still before you begin grooming.

2 Using a soft bristle brush, take long, gentle strokes and groom the animal from head to tail. Rhythmic movements will help to keep your pet relaxed.

PET HYGIENE

Following these basic guidelines will not only keep your home free of pet odours and pests, but will also do much to improve your pet's health. Trials show that hygiene contributes as much to disease control in animals as repeat vaccinations do. It will add to your personal enjoyment of your home, too, as well as protecting family and visitors from the potential hazards of exposure to animal parasites. Train your dog at as young an age as possible not to jump onto furniture – remember that they are pack animals who need to know who is top dog! Cats are more difficult, but give them their own comfortable sleeping area and encourage them to lie there, rather than on chairs, sofas, or beds, or shut doors to rooms you do not want them to enter.

A quick and effortless way to remove pet hairs from upholstery is with a tape-roller.

INSIDE THE HOME

As well as fleas, there are other diseases that humans can catch from pets, including roundworms, hookworms, and tapeworms, which are all transmittable from pets to their owners. This advice will keep the home you share with your pets germ-free.

WORM REGULARLY
Worm your pets regularly according to size, to eliminate parasites (roundworms).

WASH YOUR HANDS
Never touch a dog or cat while eating, and wash hands before meals and snacks if you have been stroking animals.

PET BEDDING
Pets carry bacteria that can make humans sick: keep pet bedding, dishes, and toys out of the kitchen, and away from cooking utensils or work surfaces. Sprinkle dried pennyroyal or wormwood into your pet's bed to keep it flea-free. Vacuuming around the bedding daily will pick up fleas

at adult and egg stage: empty the contents of the bag afterwards and seal in your outside bin. Wash your pet's bedding regularly.

VACUUM CARPETS
Vacuum carpets regularly to avoid the accumulation of pet hairs, especially if you have young children who spend a lot of their time on the floor.

CAT LITTER TRAYS
Two potentially serious infections, toxoplasmosis and toxocariasis (*see opposite*), can be caught from cat faeces. Keep soiled litter trays away from children and pregnant women, and wash your hands after emptying.

STORING PET FOOD
Keep opened cans of pet food in the refrigerator and cover with a reusable, plastic lid to prevent odours from contaminating other fresh foods in the fridge.

FLIES
It is important to keep houseflies and other insects out of the house, and especially away from food, since they may carry faecal matter from your pets' droppings. To deter flies, grow herbs like rue or tansy and hang bunches of them in living areas. A tub of mint by the kitchen door is also effective.

ELIMINATING ODOURS

If a cat urinates or sprays in the house, first wash the area immediately with a non-biological washing powder, and rinse thoroughly with cool water. By eliminating the smell completely you will prevent the animal from returning to the same spot to repeat the offence. Baking soda will also reduce odours when sprinkled into a cat litter tray.

If the cages of small mammals such as hamsters, guinea pigs, and ferrets smell bad, sprinkle a layer of baking soda under the bedding every time you clean out the cage.

If a puppy wets the carpet, soak the area at once with soda water, then mop up with a wet cloth, re-dampen with soda water and wipe clean.

DOG FOULING

Million of gallons of dog urine and tonnes of dog faeces are deposited on our city streets every day. The faeces of both dogs and cats contain a roundworm called *Toxocara*. This can infect humans with a disease called toxocariasis that can cause blindness or partial loss of vision. Children are the ones most obviously at risk, and must be taught as early as possible not to go near or touch pet excreta.

Sprinkle baking soda or borax on carpets and allow it to soak up the moisture and deodorize the patch.

- Have a poop-scoop handy for cleaning up mess in the garden, and for when you take your dog out in public places.
- Worm your pet regularly to ensure that its faeces are free of parasites. Look out for little white worms, like rice grains, in faeces in the summer. These flea tapeworms can be passed on to children and must be got rid of.
- Take a supply of small plastic bags for poop-scooping when you walk the dog in the street or the park; simply put your hand into the bag like a glove, pick up the faeces, pull the neck of the bag back over your hand, and twist the top closed. Many parks and local authorities provide separate bins for disposing of dog mess.
- Pregnant women should wear rubber gloves if they have to clean up dog or cat mess, because of the risk of toxocariasis and toxoplasmosis.
- Clean up pet mess as soon as possible, and use a mild disinfectant such as "soft chemistry" bleach on the area to kill off any worm eggs.

Never allow your pet on areas where children play: children can pick up roundworms from dog faeces, which gives them toxocariasis, causing cysts in the eyes and even blindness.

WORKING AT HOME

When you are setting up a workstation at home it is worth giving some careful thought to the office environment: it will contribute to the quality of your work output, as well as to your health. Make the most of whatever space you can put aside for a home office and invest in natural materials and the best possible equipment, and it will pay dividends. Try also to create a well-ventilated room with clean air for your health and well-being, and invest in effective task lighting to prevent eyestrain.

STRESS RELIEF

Long hours at work induce stress, so build regular stretches and exercise into your daily schedule. Your work will improve as a result: the brain needs rest as much as it does stimulation, and it also needs oxygen, so a brisk walk or exercise in the fresh air will improve concentration and motivation. Working at home can be both more productive and enjoyable when you look after your body. A well-designed chair and workstation is integral to this, so take time to plan the layout of your work area.

RECYCLING OFFICE EQUIPMENT

Running a home office that is environmentally friendly makes sense: buy recycled or recyclable equipment, and organize recycling bins for waste materials. Use as many non-toxic products as possible, and minimize the amount of energy spent on lighting and heating. Use your purchasing power in your choice of office supplies, and become an ethical consumer.

Create a comfortable, well-planned home office with good lighting, pale restful colours, and privacy.

Cleaning the keyboard p156

Keeping your desk tidy p157

Sitting correctly p159

Spending ethically p161

DESIGNING A HOME OFFICE

A well-designed home office is also an efficient and energy-saving one. Start by measuring the dimensions of the room, and make a floor plan that includes the position of the windows (and therefore the direction of natural light) and the position of electric and telephone points. Then plan out how to maximize your space. For example, an L-shaped desk placed in a corner ensures good access to reference items placed on shelves on the walls above the desk. Bear the following design points in mind to help you arrive at a successful solution.

SPACE

To make working at home a pleasure rather than a source of frustration, spend time planning the space and consider the following points for a satisfactory result.

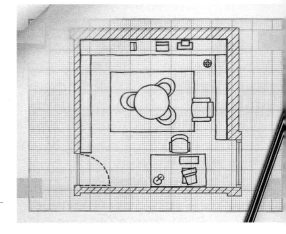

For the most efficient arrangement, draw a scale plan of the room, then plot the layout of furniture and fittings to make best use of the available space and light.

● Position the main work surface near natural light, but not in direct sunlight. Organize directional lights to suit your specific work tasks (*see opposite*).

● Ask a professional electrician to fit extra power points to ensure that your power supply is sufficient for your needs.

● Install a second phone line if you need a modem connection, or an ISDN line to access the internet at high speeds.

● Plan holes for equipment cables in work surfaces to save lengths of untidy wiring.

● Choose a soft rather than hard natural flooring material to absorb sound.

● Plan a storage area using storage cubes under work surfaces, drawers and shelving, filing cabinets and cupboards, so that all items can be put away to create a clutter-free work environment. Store box files and filing trays on deep shelves in order to keep your work surface clear.

● Keep equipment and files that you use most frequently within easy reach (on shelves above and below the worktop) and place less frequently used items further away.

● Keep worktops free of equipment such as telephones and faxes. Position these to one side so that you have space to spread out paperwork.

● The colours you choose for the office are thought to affect performance. Reds and oranges are stimulating, soft blues boost imagination and creativity, and yellow is a lively colour and is associated with mental clarity.

AIR QUALITY

According to various academic studies, photocopiers, computers, fax machines, and printers release ozone, which can exacerbate allergic reactions and make asthma worse. Ozone causes a significant reduction in lung function, yet levels close to electrical equipment in office buildings often exceed World Health Organization exposure limits. Also, office products such as adhesives and sealants contain hydrocarbon solvents that are dangerously toxic. As a general rule, choose office items made from hard rather than soft plastics, which tend to "off-gas" for long periods, sometimes with no warning smell.

ENVIRONMENT

A working environment that is comfortable and relaxed, with good levels of natural daylight, will be both more pleasant to work in and better for your productivity. Here are some hints and tips for creating that environment.

- Make your home office a strictly no-smoking zone.
- Ventilate the room well with plenty of fresh air, and/or an extractor fan.
- Install an ionizer: the balance of positive and negative ions in the atmosphere is disturbed by electronic equipment.
- Use soy-based or other non-toxic inks for printing (*see Resources page 174*).
- Use water-based marker pens and correction fluid.
- Install office furniture that will not "off-gas" and toxify the atmosphere: buy second-hand or choose natural materials other than plastics, and avoid pressed-wood products (*see page 11*). Solid wood worktops are both practical and beautiful.
- Make sure your photocopier is the "dry copy" variety and does not use volatile toners that give off strong vapours of ammonia, ethanol, and kerosene (in fact, only old or second-hand copiers are likely to do so). Maintain your copier correctly, and place it near a window to ensure good ventilation. The same applies to fax machines and laser printers. If your photocopier gives off chlorine or sulphur smells, have it serviced immediately.
- Power your office with electricity from renewable sources. Set your heating at a constant temperature, lowering it towards the end of the working day. An ambient temperature of around 15–18°C (60–64°F) is most likely to keep you alert, but remember that your body temperature drops if you sit still for long periods of time.

LIGHTING

The Applied Psychology Unit at Cambridge University in the UK has shown that good lighting leads to increased efficiency in the workplace. Here's how to achieve it.

- Make the best use possible of whatever natural light is available. If your office is in an attic room under the roof eaves, consider installing a skylight or dormer window, which will give a wonderful, even light all day long.
- To save energy, install energy-efficient light bulbs, using daylight bulbs or compact fluorescent lighting (*see page 21*), not regular fluorescent strips that can contribute to eyestrain, headaches, and stress.
- Arrange task lighting carefully for work areas.
- Lighting costs can account for 25 per cent of business electricity bills, so energy-saving bulbs can cut costs significantly. A large company cut its lighting use by up to 90 per cent in this way, and within two years they had a 53 per cent return on their investment.
- Install occupancy sensors that turn off lights when no one is in the room, or do this manually.

If possible, situate your desk next to a large window so that you can gain maximum benefit from natural light throughout the working day.

CHOOSING EQUIPMENT

When you purchase new office equipment, do find out whether it has been tested and certified to produce only low emissions. Printers and copiers can be sources of ozone and VOCs. Also bear in mind the following points.

COMPUTERS & PHOTOCOPIERS

- To save power, use the computer stand-by facility.
- Use a screen saver to save energy when your computer is not in constant use.
- Buy a printer that prints on both sides of the paper.
- Buy a copier with a duplex function (one that will photocopy on both sides of the paper).

- Buy a photocopier whose parts can be recovered and reused: in 1998 the Xerox Corporation recycled or refurbished more than 72,000 tonnes of old machines.
- Buy remanufactured or refillable toner cartridges for your copier.
- Do not sit too close to the copier, so as not to inhale fumes.

OFFICE TELEPHONES

- Purchase a telephone unit from one of the few companies that remanufactures new phones from recycled parts, (*see Resources page 174*).
- Consider setting up a business contract with a telephone company that not only offers savings on phone calls and internet use but also donates some of its company profits to ethical and environmental causes (*see Resources page 174*).

MAINTAINING EQUIPMENT

Clean out dust and other dirt particles from between the keyboards with a damp cotton bud dipped in baking soda.

Looking after your office machines carefully will give them a longer and more efficient working life, which in turn will help reduce the mountains of obsolete appliances that are difficult to recycle and often end up in landfill sites.

- Buy "soft chemistry" cleaners in bulk for office use (*see Resources page 174*).
- Wipe the computer screen clean with an anti-static cloth to keep it dust-free and to prevent eye strain.
- Wipe the office telephone clean, especially the receiver, with a "soft chemistry" lemon-based cleaner (*see Resources page 174*).
- To clean computer keyboards and telephone keypads, first unplug them, and then clean them with a dry, soft bristle brush, rubbing the bristles against your hand first to create static electricity, which will attract the dust to the bristles.
- Dirt that collects on the computer mouse mat can get inside the mouse and stop it from working correctly. Keep the mouse mat clean by wrapping some adhesive tape, sticky side out, around your fingertips, and swiping them over the surface of the mat.

CHOOSING STATIONERY

Recycled stationery supplies are now mainstream products, and no longer difficult to obtain. Many companies offer a mail-order service, and buying in bulk is not only cheaper but saves on packaging too.

- Use recycled, unbleached stationery (*see Resources page 174*) for your correspondence: it requires no raw material, cuts energy consumption, and reduces air and water pollution by up to 50 per cent.
- Some laser printer paper contains a melted plastic toner and is not valuable for recycling because it does not make quality paper the second time around. Buy plain, uncoated laser printer paper if possible.
- Think before you print a document: re-read and check the spelling to avoid running out innumerable versions that waste paper.

- Look for recycled office supplies such as scissors and pencils (*see Resources page 174*).
- Buy recyclable fax paper, mailing labels, files and document wallets, flip charts, storage boxes, and sticky notes.
- Buy refillable highlighter pens, and ink pens that use cornstarch powder (*see Resources page 174*).
- Buy office supplies in bulk where possible to reduce packaging and transport costs: consider sharing an order of office supplies with a friend or neighbouring colleague. Buying in bulk is cheaper too.

Keep a good supply of recycled address labels so that you can reuse any size of envelope that you receive.

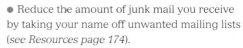

- Reduce the amount of junk mail you receive by taking your name off unwanted mailing lists (*see Resources page 174*).
- Reduce or eliminate the use of coloured paper as it is more difficult to recycle.
- Use shredded waste paper for protective packaging rather than plastic bubble-wrap.
- Take a canvas bag with you when buying office supplies.
- Use both sides of the paper for rough drafts.
- Use scrap paper for lists and memos.
- Put aside a space to store used envelopes, boxes, and padded bags for reuse.
- Use string to tie packages rather than large quantities of plastic parcel tape.
- Reuse files and ring binders, relabelling them for their new function.
- Recycle all your waste paper.
- Do research on-line or in libraries rather than ordering hard-copy material.

Instead of buying plastic desk-tidies for pens, paper clips, and other desk accessories, improvise with recycled storage tins, glassware, and coffee mugs.

CREATING A WORKSTATION

Using computers for long, unbroken periods of time has been shown to cause serious eyestrain, skin problems, headaches, repetitive strain injury (RSI), and high levels of stress, as well as muscular aches and pains (*see below*). Computers generate low levels of radiation, and the positively charged field around a computer neutralizes negative ions in the atmosphere. High concentrations of positive ions are associated with respiratory problems, fatigue, headaches, irritability, and metabolic disorders. Studies at Columbia University in New York have shown that people who work with VDUs all day have more physical and mental health problems.

Attach a screen-shield to a computer screen to reduce exposure to electric field radiation.

WORKING AT A COMPUTER

Computers are part of modern life and there is no avoiding them; however, how, and how much we use them will make a considerable difference to any detrimental effects they may have on us or on our working environment.

● Spend no more than four hours a day seated in front of a computer looking at the screen.
● Take a break to exercise and stretch the body every 30 minutes: exercise boosts energy levels, and the break from concentration can refresh the mind.
● Take a relaxing "eye-break" every 10 minutes: gaze into the distance, or let your eyes wander around the room.
● Use a laptop with a LCD (liquid crystal display) screen, which operates on a lower voltage, and extends its radiation less far.
● Sit as far away as possible from the screen – at least 75cm (30in) from the front of your computer.
● An anti-glare screen will also shield you from the electric fields (VLF/ELF) in electromagnetic (EMF) radiation and eliminate static.
● To reduce glare, diffused office lighting is best. Make sure that light is not shining directly onto your screen. Task lighting can be designed to illuminate your worktop without reflecting in the screen.
● Have a mobile keyboard so that you can alter its position regularly, and thus avoid repetitive strain on your wrists.

Use a towel for support rather than letting your wrists rest on the hard edge of the desk, which can be uncomfortable.

SEATING ARRANGEMENTS

A chair that supports you properly while you work is one of the most important items that you can invest in. Sitting at a PC positioned at the wrong height for your chair can strain the neck badly, and an ill-designed seat can strain your spine. A keyboard at the wrong height can create shoulder, elbow, and wrist problems.

- Invest in a quality chair with an adjustable lumbar support: your alignment changes throughout the day. Buy one with multiple adjustments for pelvic, lumbar, and shoulder support.
- Arrange your workstation so that your eyeline is level with the top of the computer monitor. The worktop height should be arranged so that your arms are relaxed, making a 90° angle with the keyboard. Your feet should be flat on the floor, and your knees bent at a 90° angle. The keyboard should be slightly slanted and wrists supported.
- Take short breaks from the PC in order to stretch and relieve stresses on the body. Working for long, unrelieved periods on a keyboard can cause repetitive strain injury (carpal tunnel syndrome), which is excruciatingly painful and debilitating. The only cure for it is rest, so it is best to avoid it in the first place.

> ### HOME DISCIPLINE
>
> Having a home office may entice you into working longer hours simply because the work is there for you to do. Be disciplined and make a point of organizing your time to take breaks, see your friends, and pursue other interests.

LOOK AFTER YOUR BODY

Take up yoga and go to a class at least once a week to help you stretch and relax. Go for regular walks. Take a short break to stretch and breathe deeply every 30 minutes.

1. Interlock your fingers and stretch your arms over your head, palms upwards. Lean back in the chair, stretch up to the ceiling, and take several deep breaths.

2. Stretch the arms out to the side of your body and point the fingers up to the ceiling. Take several deep breaths. This opens up the carpal tunnel in the wrists and helps prevent strain.

RELAXATION TECHNIQUES

Close your eyes. Massage the bridge of the nose with your index finger, working in small circles in both directions. Pinch the bridge of the nose several times. Press the fingertips gently over the closed lids. Press into the inner corners of the eyes to release tension. Massage the cheekbones with the fingertips, using a series of small circular movements.

A chair with adjustment levers to alter the height of the seat and back position will offer the best comfort and support.

MONEY MATTERS

Becoming an ethical consumer is part and parcel of questioning where things originate and how the global economy works and how it affects individual communities. Knowledge is power, and with a little economic information, thought, and reorganization we can make sure that our purchasing habits have a positive rather than a detrimental effect on the world around us. One of those ways is by buying products that carry the "Fair Trade" label.

Carpet production is one area where fair trade benefits the workers – look for the Rugmark label on handwoven rugs as a sign that they are fairly traded.

FAIR TRADE

The vast bulk of worldwide trade is controlled by multinational companies. Individual farmers and workers, particularly in developing countries, find it increasingly difficult to produce their goods independently of this system, in which profits go to the company and not to the workers, and working conditions and wages are beyond the workers' control.

There are now alternative trading organizations around the globe that campaign for human rights and give small producers access to Western markets, and enable them to sell a wide range of goods, including coffee beans and clothes. Local people group together to form cooperatives and earn a reasonable return on their products. They are guaranteed fair wages, decent working conditions, fair prices for their goods, and job security. Look out for "Traidcraft" and other fair trade labels: some goods can be found in the supermarket, wholefood and health shops, and some charity shops. Most fair trade schemes are ecologically sound, being small and efficient enterprises that use local resources and cause little pollution. Profits tend to be reinvested into the community, building health clinics and supporting other community projects.

ETHICAL INVESTMENT

This is not a new idea: ethical investment has been practised since the nineteenth century when wealthy religious groups sought to ensure that their money was not used to fund tobacco, gambling, or alcohol production, or to support those that manufactured armaments. Many major financial companies have responded to consumer demand by creating socially responsible investment funds. These funds aim to avoid harmful enterprises, while others actively support ethical ventures. There are numerous organizations that will invest your money in socially responsible ways, and financial advisers who specialize in these areas (*see Resources page 174*). Research and analysis has shown that in the long term ethical investment funds perform just as well, if not better, than other funds, as the fund managers have in-depth knowledge of the companies and why they have ethical status.

FINANCIAL INVESTMENT

● Get independent financial advice: the commission charged on investments is the same if you buy the product direct, so take this opportunity to get ethical investment advice as part of the financial service.

● Discuss your ethical viewpoint with your financial adviser in order to obtain the best product from your standpoint: environmental investment is complex and varies widely in performance.

● Consider a portfolio that may include both ethical and regular investments, in order to make the most of your savings and spread your risk.

● If your ethical investor charges a fee, make sure that the commission is fed back into your investment: you should never have to pay both a fee and a commission.

CREDIT UNIONS

● If you are unhappy with banking systems, use a local credit union where you can save and borrow money at low rates of interest in a cooperative, non-profit organization (*Resources page 174*).

● Apply for a Greenpeace credit card (PVC-free and biodegradable), knowing that a small percentage of your everyday spending will go to good causes.

● Join a local exchange and trading scheme where members exchange and share goods and services with each other. No money changes hands, and it builds up community ties as well as being a practical way of

Buying fruit and vegetables that are grown locally makes good money sense.

pooling resources and minimizing environmental impact: for example, sharing DIY tools (*see Resources pages 174*).

MORTGAGES

● Some building societies offer "green" mortgages and even commit to planting trees, as well as providing free, energy-efficiency building surveys. Others are dedicated to improving the environment by promoting sustainable housing, energy-efficient homes, and restoration of old buildings, and may even offer schemes to encourage you to grow your own organic food.

INSURANCE

● Some insurance brokers offer ethical household, travel and commercial insurance: consult an adviser or search the internet.

Support small farmers and businesses by buying goods direct from the producer so that you know their origin.

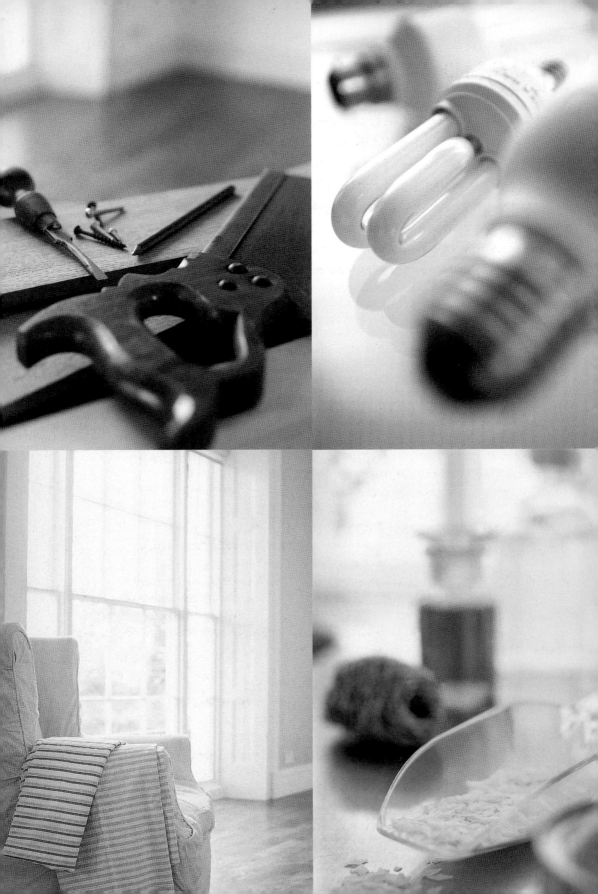

RESOURCES

One of the best ways of obtaining the most up-to-date and relevant information about the non-toxic household products on the market and the environmental issues discussed in this book is through the internet. Even if you do not have a website address for a relevant site, simply type a key word into a search-engine and it should come up with several results that match your request. Most good websites offer links to other sites that may prove surprisingly useful. So whether you want to know more about recycling matters, or house interiors, or even everyday domestic tasks, go online, or contact the associations and companies listed below by email, telephone, or letter.

HOME BASICS

Air Pollution and Health Information Pack
Emma Jenkins
693D Skipton House, Elephant & Castle,
80 London Road, London SE1 6LH
www.doh.gov.uk
Department of Health information pack on air quality issues, contact organizations, etc.

Asbestos Removal Contractors Association (ARCA)
Friars House, 6 Parkway, Chelmsford,
Essex CM1 1BE.
Tel: 01245 259 744
www.arca.org.uk
Specialist contractors for the safe removal of asbestos and other hazardous materials.

Association for Environment Conscious Building (AECB)
PO Box 32
Llandysul SA44 5ZA
Tel: 01559 370 908
Email: admin@aecb.net
www.aecb.net
For comprehensive advice and information pack on environmentally responsible practices in building.

Bathstore.com
Tel: 020 8773 5000
www.bathstore.com
For low-flush and dual-flush toilets, and water-saving showerheads.

Centre for Alternative Technology
Machynlleth,
Powys,
Wales SY20 9AZ
Tel: 01654 702 400
Email: help@catinfo.demon.co.uk
www.cat.org.uk
Advice on sustainable solutions, large range of books and products, resource guides, tip sheets; includes information on compost toilets and dual-flush systems, and greywater recycling.

Ecoconstruct
16 Great Guildford Street,
London SE1 OHS
Tel: 020 7450 2211
Email: info@ecoconstruct.com
www.constructionresources.com
For full range of natural building materials, insulation, flooring, natural paints and finishes.

Ecomerchant
Head Hill Road, Goodnestone,
nr. Faversham, Kent ME13 9BY
Tel: 01795 530 130
Email: sales@ecomerchant.co.uk
www.ecomerchant.demon.co.uk
For natural building materials, insulation,
flooring, and reclaimed products such as
doors, windows, and bathroom fittings.

Green Building Store
11 Huddersfield Road, Meltham,
Huddersfield,
West Yorkshire HD7 3NJ
Tel: 01484 854 898
Email: sales@greenbuildingstore.co.uk
www.ecoproducts.co.uk
Sustainable building products, including
PVC-free windows, doorsets, conservatories,
and non-toxic finishes.

Lead Safe Home
Tel: 0131 669 8770
www.leadsafehome.org.uk
Information on lead pollution, advice,
lead testing service.

The London Hazards Centre
308 Grays Inn Road,
London WC1 8DS
Tel: 020 7794 5999
Email: mail@lhc.org.uk
www.lhc.org.uk
For useful publications and general
background on dangerous chemicals,
asbestos, etc.

National Radiation Protection Board
Chilton,
Didcot,
Oxon 0X11 0RQ
Tel: 0800 614 529
www.nrpb.org.uk/radon
Information on radon, radon measurement
services and advice.

UK National Air Quality Information Archive
Free helpline: 0800 556 677
Email: aqinfo@aeat.co.uk
Air pollution information service.

OTHER USEFUL WEBSITES
www.epa.gov
US Environmental Protection Agency
website; includes information on lead,
radon, formaldehyde, asbestos, air quality,
water quality.

www.theconservationshop.com
www.natural-building.co.uk
www.newbuilder.co.uk
For sustainable building products.

www.aerias.org
Informative US website on air quality issues.

www.powerwatch.org
Information on EMFs and testing services.

www.metcheck.co.uk
For domestic hygrometers.

www.nsc.org
Online library that covers facts on a range of
chemicals, including formaldehyde.

● For natural non-toxic paints and finishes.
See DECORATING & FURNISHING.

SAVING ENERGY

Apollo Energy Research Ltd
Head Office,
PO Box 200,
Horley,
Surrey RH6 7FU
Tel : 01293 776 974
Email: c-hawkes@apollo-energy.com
Web: www.apollo-energy.com
For thermo-foil heat reflecting membrane.

Centre for Environmentally
Responsible Tourism
PO Box 14, Benfleet,
Essex SS7 3LW
Tel: 01268 752 827
www.c-e-r-t.org
Information packs available and advice.

B&Q
Tel: 023 8025 6256
www.diy.com
*For Climaflex, a low-cost thermoplastic
product for insulating pipes.*

CityDiesel
Email: info@futura-petroleium.com
www.futura-petroleum.com
*Environmentally friendly reformulated
diesel fuel.*

Marlec Engineering Co. Ltd
Rutland House, Trevithick Road, Corby,
Northants NN17 5XY
Tel: 01536 201 588
Email: sales@ marlec.co.uk
www.marlec.co.uk
For solar panels, wind chargers, etc.

Solartwin Ltd
15 King Street, Chester CH1 2AH
Tel: 01244 403 404
Email: hi@solartwin.com
www.solartwin.com
For solar water heating systems.

OTHER USEFUL WEBSITES
www.eta.co.uk
www.greenglobe21.com
For eco-travel.

www.saveenergy.co.uk
www.est.org.uk
www.foe.co.uk
www.realgoods.com
For general advice on saving energy.

www.nationalcarshare.co.uk
For car sharing.

● For natural insulation materials.
See HOME BASICS.

DECORATING & FURNISHING

Alphabeds
92 Tottenham Court Road,
London W1T 4TL
Tel: 020 7636 6840
Email: enquiries@alphabeds.co.uk
www.alphabeds.co.uk
For natural beds, mattresses, and futons.

Auro Organic Paint Supplies
Unit 2, Pamphillions Farm, Purton End,
Debden, Saffron Walden,
Essex CB11 3JT
Tel: 01799 543 077
Email: sales@auroorganic.co.uk
www.auroorganic.co.uk
For natural paints and finishes by mail order.

Ecospaints
Unit 34, Heysham Business Park,
Middleton Road, Heysham,
Lancashire LA33PP
Tel: 01524 852 371
Email: lakelandpaints@btconnect.com
www.ecospaints.com
For natural paints and finishes.

Eco Solutions Ltd
Summerleaze House, Church Road,
Winscombe,
North Somerset BS25 1BH
Tel: 01934 844 484
Email: info@ecosolutions.co.uk
www.ecosolutions.co.uk
*For natural paint removal products;
painted wallpaper remover.*

Francesca Lime Wash Ltd
Battersea Business Centre,
99–109 Lavender Hill,
London SW11 5QL
Tel: 020 7228 7694
Email: francesca@francescaspaint.com
www.francescaspaint.com
For natural paints and finishes.

Healthy House
Cold Harbour, Ruscombe, Stroud,
Gloucestershire GL6 6DA
Tel: 01453 752 216
Email: info@healthy-house.co.uk
www.healthy-house.co.uk
*For natural fabrics, clothes, and
household textiles.*

The Green Shop
Bisley,
Stroud,
Gloucesershire GL6 7BX
Tel: 01452 770 629
Email: enquiries@greenshop.co.uk
www.greenshop.co.uk
For natural paints and finishes.

Greenfibres
Freepost LON 7805,
Totnes,
Devon TQ9 5ZZ
Tel: 01803 868 001
Email: mail@greenfibres.com
www.greenfibres.com
*For natural fabrics, clothes, household
textiles, including bedlinen.*

One Village
Charlbury,
Oxfordshire OX7 3SQ
Email: progress@onevillage.co.uk
www.onevillage.co.uk
Tel: 0845 4584 7070
*Fair trade organization; for household
goods, including rugs.*

Natural Collection
Eco House, Monmouth Place,
Bath BA12DQ
Tel: 0870 331 3333
Email: info@naturalcollection.com
www.naturalcollection.com
For natural household textiles, and clothes.

Textiles From Nature
84 Stoke Newington Church Street,
London N16 OAP
Tel: 020 7241 0990
Email: jag@textilesfromnature.com
www.textilesfromnature.com
*For natural fabrics, including hemp and
jute, clothes, and household textiles.*

OTHER USEFUL WEBSITES
www.epa.gov
Information on volatile organic compounds.

www.paint.org/leftoverpaint.htm
For advice on disposing of leftover paint.

● For listings of paints, finishes, and natural
furnishings. See HOME BASICS.

CLEANING THE HOME

Centre for Alternative Technology
See HOME BASICS
*For natural beech brushes, septic tank
conditioner, and drain cleaner.*

Ecover
c/o Beasley and Christopher
21 Castle Street, Brighton BN1 2HD
Tel: 01273 206 997
Email: jane-beasley@pavilion.co.uk
www.ecover.com
*For "soft chemistry" cleaning products,
including washing-up liquid, cream cleaner,
multi-surface cleaner, heavy-duty citrus
cleaner, floor soap, toilet cleaner, dishwasher
tablets, and rinse aid.*

Natural Collection
See HOME BASICS
For beech and bristle brushes, natural furniture polish, brass and silver cleaner.

Natural Eco Trading Ltd
PO Box 115, Tunbridge Wells, Kent TN4 8WJ
Tel: 01892 616 871
Email: info@greenbrands.co.uk
www.greenbrands.co.uk
For a wide range of cleaning products.

The London Hazards Centre
See HOME BASICS
For information on strong chemicals.

OTHER USEFUL WEBSITES
www.greenpeace.org
For general information.

www.organizedhome.com
Practical advice on many aspects of homemaking.

WASHING & LAUNDRY

Aqua Ball
21st Century Health Ltd, 2 Fitzhardinge
Street, London W1H 6EE
Tel: 020 7935 5440
Email: info@21stcenturyhealth.co.uk
www.aquaball.com
For laundry balls.

Ecover
see CLEANING THE HOME
Washing powder and liquid, bleach (made of percarbonate), water softener, liquid wool wash and fabric conditioner, and citrus cleaner for stain removal.

Retone Products
Retone House, 60 Sherborne Street,
Manchester M8 8LR
Tel: 0161 832 7788

Email: retone1123@aol.com
For stain removal.

Natural Collection
see DECORATING & FURNISHING
For natural washing products.

OTHER USEFUL WEBSITES
www.agores.org
For information on renewable energy sources.

www.mercola.com
For information on dry-cleaning.

www.ecozone.co.uk
www.greenbrands.com
For "soft chemistry" washing products.

RECYCLING WASTE

Alupro
1 Brockhill Court, Brockhill Lane,
Redditch B97 6RB
Tel: 0845 722 7722
Email: info@alupro.org.uk
www.alupro.org.uk
For recycling aluminium foil.

British Battery Manufacturers Association
26 Grosvenor Gardens,
London SW1W 0GT
Tel: 020 7838 4878
For information on recycling batteries.

Bytes Twice
SWAP, 74 Kirkgate,
Leeds, LS2 7DJ
Tel: 0113 243 8777
For recycling computers and accessories.

Directory and Yellow Pages Recycling
Tel: 0800 783 1592
www.yell.com
For recycling business directories.

European Recycling Company LTD
Whitehead House, 120 Beddington Lane
Croydon, Surrey CR9 4ND
Email: ercoltd@aol.com
For recycling footwear.

Envirocare
Freepost (SWB987), Bristol BS11 9ZY
Tel: 0845 458 8822
Email: clive@tonerdonor.co.uk
www.tonerdonor.co.uk
*Run a free collection toner donor scheme
(laserjet, inkjet, fax or copier cartridges) to
raise funds for cerebral palsy and other
disabilities. They also accept mobile phones.*

Environmental Mobile Control
Unit 3 Glansyl Way,
Hawkins Lane Industrial Estate,
Burton-on-Trent, Staffordshire DE14 1LX
Tel: 01283 516 259
Email: info@emc-recycle.com
www.emc-recycle.com
To recycle mobile phones.

Going For Green
Elizabeth House, The Pier, Wigan W23 4EX
Tel: 01942 612 621
www.encams.org
*Environmental charity for sustainable
environments; encourages local councils to
recycle Christmas trees by shredding.*

Office Green
Orchard House,
10-11 Portland Commercial Estate,
Ripple Road, Barking, Essex IG11 0TW
Collection Hotline: 0800 833 480
Email:mail@officegreen.co.uk
www.officegreen.co.uk
*Free collection for used laser and inkjet
cartridges for recyling; also collect and recycle
wide range of office machines and equipment,
including printers, mobile phones, and
computers.*

The Furniture Recycling Network
c/o C.F.S., The Old Drill Hall, 17a Vicaraage
Street North, Wakefield, Yorkshire WF1 4JS
Tel: 01924 375 252
Email furniture.rn@virgin.net
www.btinternet.com/~frn/FRN
*Co-ordinating body for furniture recycling
projects throughout the UK.*

Waste Watch
96 Tooley Street, London SE1 2TH
Tel: 0870 243 0136
Email: info@wastewatch.org.uk
www.wastewatch.org.uk
*Excellent organisation with detailed contacts
and information, with by far the best recycle-
dedicated website for recyling household
electrical or electronic waste, mobile phones,
CFC extraction from fridges, etc.*

OTHER USEFUL WEBSITES
www.camcnty.gov.uk
www.useitagain.org.uk
www.crn.org.uk
www.doingyourbit.org.uk
www.recycle.mcmail.com
*For awareness, initiatives and information,
plus useful contacts.*

www.obviously.com
www.virtualrecycling.com
www.ecorecycle.vic.gov.au
www.dep.state.pa.us
www.epa.gov
Useful information on recycling.

www.nike.com
*For details of reuse-a-shoe program
in the USA.*

www.happychild.org.uk
ublib.buffalo.edu/libraries/units/hsl/cms/
   donationprograms.html
*Details of charities, schools, etc, requiring
books.*

HEALTHY FOOD

Earthcare Ltd
48 Queens Road, Coventry CV1 3EH,
Tel: 024 7663 0832
Email: info@solvita.co.uk
www.solvita.co.uk
Offers a range of soil testing kits.

The Fairtrade Foundation
Suite 204, 16 Baldwin's Gardens,
London EC1N 7RJ
Tel: 020 7405 5942
Email: mail@fairtrade.org.uk
www.fairtrade.org.uk
Works for better terms of trade and decent production conditions in developing countries; over 80 different products available in most major supermarkets, Fair Trade shops, and by mail order.

The Fresh Food Company Ltd
The Orchard, 50 Wormholt Road,
London W12 0LS
Tel: 020 8749 8778
Email: organics@freshfood.co.uk
www.freshfood.co.uk
For nationwide delivery of organic food.

National Association of Farmers' Markets
South Vaults, Green Park Station,
Green Park Road, Bath B1 1JB
Tel: 01225 787 914
Email: nafm@farmersmarkets.net
www.farmersmarkets.net
For a list of farmers' markets countrywide.

Organics Direct
Olympic House, 196 The Broadway,
Wimbledon, London SW19 1SN
Tel: 020 8545 7676
Email: info@organicsdirect.co.uk
www.organicsdirect.co.uk
For nationwide delivery of organic food.

The Organic Shop
The Organic Shop, Freepost,
Alderley Edge,
Cheshire, SK9 7YG
Tel: 0845 674 4000
Email: info@theorganicshop.co.uk
www.theorganicshop.co.uk
For nationwide delivery of organic food.

The Organic Herb Trading Company
Court Farm, Milverton,
Somerset TA4 1NF
Tel: 01823 401 205
Email: info@hambledenherbs.co.uk
www.hambledenherbs.co.uk
For organic herbs and spices, herbal teas, and herbal tinctures.

Magic Communications PLC
5 Priors London Road
Bishops Stortford, Herts CM23 5ED
01279 755 799
Email:info@detox.co.uk
www.detox.co.uk
For reverse osmosis water purification system.

Pitfield Organic Brewery
The Beer Shop,
14 Pitfield Street,
London N1 6EY
Tel: 020 7739 3701
Email: sales@pitfieldbeershop.co.uk
www.pitfieldbeershop.co.uk
Supplies a full range of organic, vegetarian, and vegan beers by mail order.

Pureflo
Mount Pleasant Lane,
Bricket Wood, St Albans,
Herts AL2 3XD
Tel: 01923 682 774
E-mail: enquiries@pureflo.co.uk
www.pureflo.co.uk
For a range of water filters.

The Pure Wine Company
Unit 18, Woods Browning Industrial Estate,
Respirin Road, Bodmin,
Cornwall PL31 1DQ
Tel: 01208 77219
Email: service@purewine.co.uk
www.purewine.co.uk
*For delivery of organic, vegetarian, and
vegan wines throughout the UK.*

Savant Distribution Ltd
15 Iveson Approach,
Leeds LS16 6LJ
Tel: 0845 0606070
Email: info@savant-health.com
www.savant-health.com
*For omega-3 oils and a wide range
of supplements; also a water filter.*

Simply Organic Food Company Ltd
Olympic House, 196 The Broadway,
Wimbledon, London SW19 1SN
Tel: 0845 1000 444
Email info@simplyorganic.net
www.simplyorganic .net
*For nationwide delivery of organic food,
and wines and beers.*

Swaddles Green Farm
Hare Lane, Buckland St Mary,
Chard TA20 3JR
Tel: 01460 234 387
Email: information@swaddles.co.uk
www.swaddles.co.uk
*For nationwide delivery of organic food,
including meat, poultry, and fish.*

Vintage Roots Ltd
Farley Farms, Bridge Farm,
Reading Road,
Arborfield, Berkshire RG2 9H
Tel: 0800 980 4992
www.vintageroots.co.uk
*For delivery of organic wines throughout
the UK.*

OTHER USEFUL WEBSITES
www.faia.org.uk/enumbers.htm
*For complete list of European Union
permitted additives.*

www.soilassociation.org
*Leading campaigning and certification
organisation for organic food and farming.*

PERSONAL CARE

Aveda
AVD Cosmetics
First Floor, Holborn Hall,
193–7 High Holborn,London WC1V 7DB
Tel: 020 7297 6350
www.aveda.com
*For natural skin care, hair care, make-up etc;
products containing oryzanol.*

Beauty Without Cruelty
Devonshire Road Industrial Estate,
Millom, Cumbria LA18 4JS
Tel: 01229 775185
*For information on products not tested
on animals.*

Cariad
104 Bancroft,
Hitchin, Hertfordshire SG5 1LY
Tel: 01462 443 518
Email: mailorder@cariad.co.uk
www.cariad.co.uk
*For essential oils, unscented base creams and
lotions, massage oils, and skin care and body
care products.*

Elysia Natural Skincare
Unit 19–20, Stockwood Business Park,
Stockwood, Worcestershire B96 6SX
Tel: 01386 792 622
Email: enquiries@drhauschka.co.uk
www.drhauschka.co.uk
*For Dr. Hauschka natural, biodynamic skin
care, hair care, make-up, deodorants, etc.*

Fragrant Earth
Orchard Court, Magdelene Street,
Glastonbury, Somerset BA6 9EW
Tel: 01458 831216
Email: all-enquiries@fragrant-earth.com
www.fragrant-earth.com
For pure essential oils and hydrolats.

Greenfibres
see DECORATING AND FURNISHING
For reusable organic cotton sanitary pads.

The Green People Company
Brighton Road, Handcross,
West Sussex RH17 6BZ
Tel: 01444 401444
Email: organic@greenpeople.co.uk
www.greenpeople.co.uk
For natural skin care, hair care, make-up, etc.,
and natural products for men.

House of Mistry
15–17 South End Road, Hampstead Heath,
London NW3 2PT
Tel: 020 7794 0848
Email: mistry@dial.pipex.com
www.dspace.dial.pipex.com
For neem products; also organic soap,
shampoos, ointments.

Logona
Unit 3, Beck's Green Business Park,
Beck's Green Lane, Ilketshall St Andrew,
Beccles, Suffolk NR34 8NB
Tel: 01986 781 782
Email: enquiries@logona.co.uk
www.logona.co.uk
For natural skin care, hair care,
make-up etc., men's care products.

Neals Yard Remedies
Head office: 26-34 Ingate Place,
Battersea, London SW8 3NS
Customer Service Helpline: 020 7627 1949
Email: mail@nealsyardremedies.com
www.nealsyardremedies.com
For vegetable soaps, green clay, natural skin
care, oral hygiene, bodycare, deodorant
stones, hair care; also essential oils,
homeopathic remedies, herbal tinctures, and
vegetable base oils.

NHR Organic Oils
5 College Terrace,
Brighton BN2 0EE
Tel: 0845 310 8066
Email: organic@nhr.kz
www.nhr.kz
For organic and wild-grown essential oils.

Organic Botanics
PO Box 2140,
Hove BN3 5BX
Tel: 01273 773 182
www.organicbotanics.com
For natural skin care, body care, and
hair care.

Simply Organic
see HEALTHY FOOD
For organic cotton sanitary pads.

Suma Wholefoods
Lacy Way,
Lowfields Industrial Park
Elland, West Yorkshire HX5 9DB
Tel: 0845 458 2291
Email: sales@suma.co.uk
www.suma.co.uk
For unbleached, dioxin-free, recycled tissues,
toilet paper, etc.

Weleda (UK) Ltd
Heanor Road, Ilkeston,
Derbyshire DE7 8DR
Tel: 0115 944 8200
Email: weledauk@compuserve.com
www.weleda.co.uk
For natural skin care, hair care, body care,
men's care products, dental care.

www.colipa.com/eu_cosmetics.html
The European Cosmetic Toiletry and Perfumery Association; details of EU cosmetics directive.

www.perfectnails.uk.com
www.clinique.co.uk
For formaldehyde- and toluene-free nail products.

NATURAL REMEDIES

Ainsworths Homeopathic Pharmacy
36 New Cavendish Street, London W1M 7LH
Tel: 020 7935 5330
Email: mark.ainsworths@ukonline.co.uk
www.ainsworths.com
For homeopathic remedies.

Bioforce (UK) Ltd
2 Brewster Place, Irvine, Ayrshire KA11 5DD
Tel: 01294 277 344
Email: enquiries@bioforce.co.uk
www.bioforce.co.uk
Herbal remedies and supplements.

British Acupuncture Council
63 Jeddo Road, London W12 9HQ
www.acupuncture.org.uk
Maintains a register of practitioners.

General Osteopathic Council
176 Tower Bridge Road, London SE1 3LU
www.osteopathy.org.uk
Offers advice on finding a practitioner.

Homeopathic Medical Association
6 Livingstone Road,
Gravesend, Kent DA12 5DZ
Tel: 01474 560 336
Email: info@the-hma.org
www.the-hma.org
Information about homeopathic medicine, and lists of practitioners.

Helios Homeopathic Pharmacy
97 Camden Road, Royal Tunbridge Wells,
Kent TN1 2QR
Tel: 01892 537 254
Email: pharmacy@helios.co.uk
www.helios.co.uk
For a wide range of homoepathic remedies.

National Institute of Medical Herbalists
56 Longbrook Street, Exeter,
Devon EX4 6AH
Tel: 01392 426 022
Email:nimh@ukexeter.freeserve.co.uk
www.nimh.org.uk
Maintains a list of practitioners.

Society of Teachers of the Alexander Technique
129 Camden Mews, London NW1 9AH
www.stat.org.uk
Maintains a register of practitioners.

www.naturesbestonline.com
For herbal supplementsvitamins, and minerals.

www.lichtwer.co.uk
Herbal supplements.

www.aloeveracentre.co.uk
Nutritional drinks, skin care products, beauty care and cosmetics.

www.bwy.org
For details of local yoga classes.

BABYCARE

Green Baby
345 Upper Street, London NI OPD
Tel: 020 7226 4345
Email: jill@greenbaby.co.uk
www.greenbaby.co.uk
For extensive range of organic babycare products, clothing, and nappies.

Greenfibres
see HEALTHY EATING
For extensive range of organic baby clothing, bedding, and cot made from sustainable wood.

House of Winkle
Offa House, Offa Street,
Hereford HR1 2LH
Tel: 01432 268 018
Email: houseofwinkle@hotmail.com
www.houseofwinkle.co.uk
Organic mattresses for cot and crib, bedding, linen.

Huggababy
19–21 Prya Centre, Talgarth,
Brecon LD3 ODS
Tel: 01874 711 629
Email: margaret@huggababy.co.uk
www.huggababy.co.uk
For extensive range of organic babycare products, baby carrier, clothing, etc.

La Leche League
24 hour helpline: 020 7242 1278
www.laleche.org.uk
Breastfeeding support.

National Association of Nappy Services
Tel: 0121 693 4949
Email: info@changeanappy.co.uk
www.changeanappy.co.uk
For information on nappy services.

Organics Direct
see HEALTHY EATING
For organic baby food.

The Real Nappy Association
PO Box 3704,
London SE6 4RX
Tel: 020 8299 4519
www.realnappy.com
For information on nappy services.

Schmidt Natural Clothing
21 Posthorn Close, Forest Row,
East Sussex RH18 5DE
Tel: 01342 822 169
Email: glenn@naturalclothing.co.uk
www.naturalclothing.co.uk
For organic cotton nappies, natural clothing for babies and children, and bedding.

SDF
60–62 Kings Road
Reading, Berkshire RG1 3AA
Tel: 0118 9510 518
Email: info@organico.co.uk
www.organico.co.uk
For Babynat organic milk formula.

Simply Organic
see HEALTHY FOOD
For organic baby food.

OTHER USEFUL WEBSITES
www.greenchoices.org
www.nappyfacts.co.uk
www.wen.org.uk
www.parentsplace.com
www.spiritofnature.co.uk

www.checnet.org
For information on environmental health risks children face in the home.

KEEPING PETS

Denes Natural Pet Care Ltd
Freepost, 2 Osmond Road, Hove East, Sussex
BN3 1BR
Tel: 01273 325 364
Email: info@denes.com
www.denes.com
For organic pet foods.

Fragrant Earth
See PERSONAL CARE
For essential oils and hydrolats.

Genitrix Ltd
Unit 25,
Station Road Industrial Estate,
Southwater,
Horsham RH13 9UD
Tel: 01403 734 555
Email: mail@genitrix.co.uk
www.genitrix.co.uk
For Xenex, a long-lasting natural insect repellant for pets.

Green Arc Animal Nutrition
Pendle House Barn,
Barley, Pendle,
Nelson BB9 6LQ
Tel: 01282 606 810
Email: greenark@zen.co.uk
www.greenark.co.uk
For organic pet foods.

Homeopathic Vets
Tel: 01367 718 115
For information on vets nationwide who are qualified by the Faculty of Homeopathy.

Pet Nutrition Concepts Ltd
PNC Ltd PO Box, Chichester,
West Sussex PO20 7YT
Tel: 01243 512 024
www.petnutrition.co.uk
For vitamins, minerals and nutraceuticals for dogs, cats, and horses.

Savant Distribution Ltd
See HEALTHY FOOD
For supplements and herbal treatments.

Traffic International
219c Huntingdon Road,
Cambridge CB3 0DL
Tel: 01223 277427
Email: traffic@trafficint.org
www.traffic.org
Monitors wildlife trade; provides access to protected species lists.

WORKING AT HOME

Association of British Credit Unions Ltd
Holyoake House, Hanover Street,
Manchester M60 0AS
Tel: 0161 832 3694
Email: info@abcul.org
www.abcul.org
Information on credit unions, and where to find your local credit unit.

The Back Shop
14 New Cavendish Street,
London W1M 7LJ
020 7935 9120
www.thebackshop.co.uk
Back care products, including office seating, workstations and equipment, and office design.

Barchester Green Investment
45 Catherine Street, FREEPOST,
Salisbury SP12UR
Tel: 0800 328 6818
Email: info@barchestergreen.co.uk
www.barchestergreen.co.uk
Advice on ethical investments.

Blue Ridge Technology
100-A Woodwind Industrial Court,
Cary, North Carolina 27511, USA
Tel: 1 800 745 5530
Email: info@blueridgetech.com
For telephones made from recycled parts.

Centre for Alternative Technology
see HOME BASICS
For non-toxic inks, recycled pencils, and scissors etc.

Computers for Charity
PO Boz 48, Bude, Cornwall EX23 8BL
Tel: 01288 361 177
Email: Cfcdonations@btinternet.com
(for leaving computers) or

Cfcadmin@btinternet.com *(for buying)*
www.computersforcharity.org.uk
To recycle computers.

Co-operative Bank
PO Box 200, Delf House,
Skelmersdale WN8 6NY
Tel: 08457 212 212
Email: jennie@co-operativebank.co.uk
www.co-operativebank.co.uk
For advice on ethical banking.

EarthCall Telecommunications Ltd
EarthCall House, Carters Hill, Toppesfield,
Halstead, Essex CO9 4LZ
Tel: 0800 068 4949
Email: info@earthcall.co.uk
www.earthcall.co.uk
For savings on your telephone and internet
bills, plus 50 per cent of the company's profits
go to its Biodiversity Fund.

The Ecology Building Society
FREEPOST 18 Station Road, Crosd Hills,
Keighley, West Yorkshire BD20 7EH
Email: info@ecology.co.uk
www.ecology.co.uk
For advice on green mortgages.

Ecover
see CLEANING THE HOME
For "soft chemistry" cleaners.

**EIRIS (Ethical Investment Research and
Information Service)**
80–84Bondway, London SW8 1SF
Tel: 020 7840 5700
Email: ethics@eiris.org
www.eiris.org
For ethical investments.

The Ethical Investment Co-operative Ltd
Vincent House, 15, Victoria Road, Darlington,
Co. Durham DL1 5SF
Tel: 01325 267 228

Email: info@ethicalmoney.org
www.ethicalmoney.org
Advice on ethical investments.

Green Stationery Company
Studio One, 114 Walcot Street, Bath BA1 5BG
Tel: 01225 480556
Email: jay@greenstat.co.uk
www.greenstat.co.uk
For recycled stationery, refillable highlighter
pens, cornstarch ink pens.

Greenpeace Visa Card
see **Co-operative Bank** *(opposite)*
PVC-free and biodegradable credit card.

LETSLINK
12 Southcote Road, London N19 5BJ
Tel: 020 7607 7852
Email: lets@letslinkuk.org
www.letslinkuk.net
For information on a local exchange and
trading schemes, or contact your local Citizens
Advice Bureau.

Lightswitch Helpline
Tel: 0870 513 3538
www.lightswitch.co.uk
Advice on criteria for finding funding for
low energy lighting, advice on fittings.

Mail Preference Service
Freepost 22, London W1E 7EZ
Tel: 020 7291 3310
Email: mps@dma.org.uk
www.mpsonline.org.uk
To stop unwanted junk mail.

Naturesave Policies Insurance
Freepost (SWB 30837)
Devon TQ9 5ZZ
Tel: 01803 864 390
Email: mail@naturesave.co.uk
www.naturesave.co.uk
For advice on ethical insurance.

New Economics Foundation
Cinnamon House, 6-8 Cole Street,
London SE1 4YK
Tel: 020 7089 2800
Email: info@neweconomics.org
www.neweconomics.org
Reports on ethical investments;
ethical criteria.

Paperback Ltd
Unit 2, Bow Triangle Business Centre,
Eleanor Street, London E3 4NP
Tel: 020 8980 5580
Email: sales@paperback.fsbusiness.co.uk
For recycled stationery.

Recycled Paper Supplies
Gate Farm, Fen End, Kenilworth CV8 1NW
Tel: 01676 533 832
Email:enquiry@recycled-paper.co.uk
www.recycled-paper.co.uk
For recycled stationery.

Remarkable Pencils
56 Glentham Road, London SW13 9JJ
Tel: 020 8741 1234
Email: info@remarkable.co.uk
www.remarkable.co.uk
For recycling cups from vending machines
into pencils.

Traidcraft
Kingsway, Gateshead,
Tyne & Wear NE11 0NE
Tel: 0191 491 0591
www.traidcraft.co.uk
UK's largest fair trade organisation.

Triodos Bank (UK)
Brunel House, 11 The Promenade,
Clifton, Bristol BS8 3NN
Tel: 0117 973 9339
Email: mail@triodos.co.uk
www.triodos.co.uk
For advice on ethical banking.

UK Cartridge Recycling Association
(UKCRA)
19b School Road, Sale,
Manchester M33 7XX
Tel: 01706 525 050
Email: info@ukra.com
www.ukcra.com
For information on recycled laser printer
cartridges.

OTHER USEFUL WEBSITES:
www.getethical.com
www.ethicalinvestment.org.uk
www.ftse4good.com
www.greenchoices.org
www.realmoney.org
www.socialinvest.org
www.coopamerica.org
Offer information and advice on ethical
investments.

www.galvins.com
For office design tips.

www.wastewatch.com
Detailed information on recycling.

www.antiglare.co.uk
For anti-glare screens.

www.yahoo.com
Keeps an updated list of recycled printer
supplies.

www.recoup.org
www.save-a-cup.co.uk
For recycling cups from vending machines.

RECOMMENDED BOOKS

Berthold-Bond, Annie, Better Basics for the Home: Simple Solutions for Less Toxic Living (Three Rivers Press, 1999)

Brown, Lynda, Planet Organic: Organic Living (Dorling Kindersley, 2000)

Brown, Lynda, The Shopper's Guide to Organic Food (Fourth Estate, 1998)

Chevallier, Andrew, Encyclopedia of Medicinal Plants (Dorling Kindersley, 2nd edition 2001)

Christensen, Karen, The Green Home (Piatkus, 1995)

Dadd, Debra Lynn, Home Safe Home: Protecting Yourself and Your Family from Everyday Toxics and Harmful Household Products in the Home (J. P. Tarcher, 1997)

Elliot, Renee J., and Treuille, Eric, The Organic Cookbook: Naturally Good Food (Dorling Kindersley, 2001)

Fairley, Josephine, Planet Organic: Organic Beauty (Dorling Kindersley, 2001)

Good Housekeeping Organic Handbook (HarperCollins, 2001)

Grant, Doris, and Joyce, Jean, Food Combining for Health: Get Fit with Foods That Don't Fight (Thorsons, 1994)

Henry Doubleday Research Association, HDRA Encyclopedia of Organic Gardening (Dorling Kindersley, 2001)

Iyengar, B.K.S., Light on Yoga (HarperCollins, New edition 2001)

Iyengar, B.K.S., Yoga: The Path to Holistic Health (Dorling Kindersley, DATE?)

Jewell, N. (Ed.), Richard Brier's Green Life Directory (Kingsley Media Ltd, 2000)

Lockie, Andrew, and Geddes, Nicola, The Complete Guide to Homeopathy (Dorling Kindersley, Revised Edition 2001)

Mendelson, Cheryl, Home Comforts: The Art and Science of Keeping House (Weidenfeld Nicolson, new edition 2002)

Scaravelli, Vanda, Awakening the Spine : The Stress-Free Yoga That Works with the Body to Restore Health, Vitality and Energy (Harper San Francisco, 1991)

Thich Nhat Hanh, The Miracle of Mindfulness (Rider Books, 1991)

Ungaro, Alycea, Pilates Body in Motion (Dorling Kindersley, 2002)

Vann, Lizzie, Planet Organic: Baby and Toddler Cookbook (Dorling Kindersley, 2000)

INDEX

A

aerosol propellant, 186
acesulfame, 91
acetate, soft furnishings, 40
acetone, 66, 122, 186
acne, 115
acrylic, soft furnishings, 40
acupuncture, 127
additives:
  in food, 96–7, 137
  in wine, 102
adhesives, 87
  removing, 69
aerosol sprays, 16, 84
aftershave, 125
AHAs (alpha-hydroxy acids), 113
ailments, natural remedies,
  127–33
air conditioning, 23
air fresheners, 16, 49, 124
air quality, 10, 16–17
  home offices, 154, 155
alcohol, 102, 115
aldehydes, 124
Alexander Technique, 127
allantoin, 114
allergies:
  bedding, 39
  children, 135
  pet care, 149
aloe vera, 131
alpha-linoleic acid (ALA), 91
aluminium:
  antacids, 130
  foil, 87
  food safety, 107
  recycling, 79
aluminium chlorohydrate, 125
amitraz, 146
ammonia, 186
animals, organic farming, 92, 94–5
antacids, 130
antibiotics, residues in food, 94–5
antifreeze, 85
ants, 60
appliances:
  cleaning, 53

energy conservation, 26–7
  recycling, 80
arnica, 131, 148
aromatherapy, 127
asbestos, 10–11
aspartame, 91, 186
asthma, 39, 135
azinphos-methyl, 93

B

baby care, 135–41
bacteria:
  food hygiene, 107
  pet hygiene, 150
  probiotics, 91
bags, waste reduction, 76, 79
baking soda, 47, 52
  cleaning appliances, 53
  cleaning bathrooms, 54, 55
  cleaning walls, 50
  as deodorant, 125
  stain removal, 51, 68
bamboo furniture, cleaning, 56
banks, 161
basins, cleaning, 54
bathing:
  body care, 118–19
  pets, 147
bathrooms:
  cleaning, 54–5
  water conservation, 15
batteries, 77, 84
beauty products see cosmetics
bedding:
  for babies, 140–1
  laundry, 39, 72
  natural fabrics, 31, 36, 38–9
  pets, 150
  synthetic fabrics, 40
beer, 102
beeswax polish, 56, 57
benzene, 42, 98, 124, 186
benzopyrene, 17
benzyl alcohol, 112
BHAs (beta-hydroxy acids), 113
bicarbonate of soda see baking
  soda

biodiversity, 100
'biological' washing powders, 70
bites, insect, 129
bladder cancer, 121
blankets, 37, 38, 39, 72
bleach, 37, 48, 66, 71
blinds, cleaning, 50
blood stains, removing, 67
body care, 118–19
bodywork, 127, 132–3
boilers, 14, 23
books, recycling, 80
borates, 13
borax, 47, 186
  bleaches, 71
  cleaning bathrooms, 55
  stain remover, 67
  timber preservatives, 13
boron, 71, 186
bottle feeding, 136
bottled water, 98
botulism, 107
brass, cleaning, 57
breast cancer, 117, 121
breastfeeding, 136
brewers' yeast, 145, 147
brushes, 47
  cleaning, 34
building materials, 11
building societies, 161

C

caffeine, 99, 115
calcium deposits, in washing
machines, 71
calendula, natural remedies, 131
campylobacter, 95
cancer, 92, 93, 96, 117, 121
candlesticks, removing wax, 59
cane furniture, cleaning, 56
cans, 79, 102
carbaryl, 146
carbohydrates, 90, 91
carbon dioxide, 19
carbon monoxide, 17
carbon water filters, 99
carnauba wax, 51, 93

carpal tunnel syndrome, 159
carpets, 42–3
  allergies, 149
  pet hygiene, 150
  stain removal, 51, 68
cars, 28–9
  hazardous waste disposal, 84–5
  reducing waste, 77, 85
casein paint, 33
cast-iron, cleaning, 57
cats, 143–51
caustic soda, 35
cellulose fibre insulation, 24
central heating, 23
ceramics, cleaning, 59
CFCs, 16, 27, 73, 187
chairs, home offices, 159
chamomile, natural remedies, 131
charity shops, 80
chemicals:
  cleaning products, 46, 48
  in cosmetics, 112–13
  residues in food, 92, 93–4
chewing gum, removing, 69
chicken, free-range, 95
chilblains, 128
children:
  allergies, 135
  baby care, 135–41
  educating about recycling, 87
  head lice, 120
  pollution and, 135
china:
  cleaning, 59
  repairs, 87
chiropractic, 127
chloramine, 98
chlorine, 48, 1187
chlorine bleach, 66, 71
chlorine dioxide, 98
chocolate stains, removing, 67
chopping boards, 52, 107
chrome, cleaning, 57
cider vinegar:
  flea deterrent, 147
  as skin toner, 116
citrate, 71
citric acid, 47
citronella, 61
citrus oils, 47
clay masks, skin care, 116

cleaning, 45–61
  bathrooms, 54–5
  cars, 29
  chemical cleaners, 48
  floors, 51
  fragrances, 49
  furniture and ornaments, 56–9
  kitchens, 52–3
  natural cleaners, 46–7
  paint brushes, 34
  toys, 141
  walls, 50
  windows, 50
cleaning products, 45
  air pollution, 16
  disposal of, 85
  natural cleaners, 46–7
cloth nappies, 138, 139
clothes:
  baby clothes, 140
  dry cleaning, 16, 73
  ironing, 73
  laundry, 26, 63–73
  moths, 60
  recycling, 80
  stain removers, 66–9
cloves, natural remedies, 131
cockroaches, 60
coconut derivatives, skin care, 114
coconut fibre insulation, 24
cod liver oil, 145
coffee, 99
  hair rinse, 121
  stain removal, 68
coir matting, 43
colds, 128
collars, flea, 146
colourings:
  in cosmetics, 113, 187
  food additives, 97
  hair dyes, 121
colours, home offices, 154
combs, flea, 147
comfrey, natural remedies, 131
complementary therapies, 127
compost, 82–3, 104
computers:
  energy conservation, 27
  home offices, 156
  recycling, 80, 81
  working at, 158

conditioners:
  fabric, 65
  hair care, 120
construction materials, 10–13
cooking:
  energy conservation, 109
  food hygiene, 107
cooperatives, fair trade, 160
copper, cleaning, 57
cork, insulation, 24
cosmetics, 111–25
  body care, 118–19
  disposal of, 85
  foot care, 123
  fragrances, 124–5
  hair care, 120–1
  hand care, 122
  labels, 112–13
  skin care, 114–17
cot mattresses, 140–1
cotton, soft furnishings, 37
cotton wool, 119
coughs, 128
crates, recycling, 81
credit cards, 161
credit unions, 161
crop rotation, vegetables, 105
Cryptosporidium, 98
crystal, cleaning, 59
crystalline deodorant stones, 125
curtains, 31
cuts, natural remedies, 129
cycling, 28

D

dairy produce, 94–5
damp problems, 17
dandruff shampoos, 120
DBP (dibutylphthalate), 113, 122
DDT, 94, 113
DEA (diethanolaminooleamide), 112
decaffeinated coffee, 99
decorating, 31–43
DEHA (di 2-ethylhexyl adipate), 108
dental care, 119, 137
deodorants, 125
DEP (diethylphthalate), 113
desks, 154

detergents, 48, 70
diazinon, 146
dichlorobenzidene, 41
dieldrin, 13, 93, 113
diesel, 28
diethyltoluamide, 61
digestive problems, 129
dimmer switches, 21
dioxins, 136, 141, 187
dishwashers, 14, 27, 48, 106
disinfectants, 48, 98
disposable goods, alternatives to, 77
disposable nappies, 138
dogs, 143–51
doormats, 45
doors, draughtproofing, 25
drainage holes, cleaning, 54
drains, cleaning, 55
draughtproofing, 25
drinks:
    coffee and tea, 99
    water, 77, 98–9
    wines and beer, 102
driving, energy conservation, 29
drugs, 130
dry cleaning, 16, 38, 73
drying laundry, 72
dust mites, 20, 39
duvets, 39
dyes:
    hair, 121
    synthetic fabrics, 41

E

E.coli, 95
E–numbers, food additives, 97
earache, 128
echinacea, natural remedies, 131
EDTA
    (ethylenediaminetetraacetic
    acid), 71, 97, 187
egg stains, removing, 67
eggs, free-range, 95
electric blankets, 27
electrical equipment:
    energy conservation, 19, 26–7
    home offices, 154
    recycling, 80
electricity:

heating systems, 17
home offices, 155
    power cuts, 109
    power lines, 10
electromagnetic frequencies
    (EMFs), 10, 27, 158
emulsifying wax, 114
energy conservation, 19–29
    appliances, 26–7
    cooking methods, 109
    heat and insulation, 22–5
    home offices, 155, 156
    lighting, 20–1
    travel, 28–9
enzymes, 'biological' washing
    powders, 70, 187
equipment, home offices, 156
essential fatty acids, 91
essential oils:
    dog flea massage oil, 147
    fragrances, 124–5
    natural cleaners, 47
    natural remedies, 131
    in pregnancy, 130
ethanol, 66, 187
ethical investment, 160–1
eucalyptus oil, 47
exchange schemes, 161
exercise:
    improving skin condition, 115
    working at home, 158, 159
extractor fans, 17, 49
eyes, working at a computer, 158

F

fabric conditioners, 65
fabrics see textiles
face, skin care, 116–17
faeces, pet hygiene, 150, 151
fair trade goods, 101, 160
farmers' markets, 100
farming, 92–5
fats, in diet, 90–1
fatty acids, 91
fax machines, 155
feminine hygiene, 119
ferrets, 151
fertilizers, 92, 93
filters, water, 99
finances, 160–1

fires, wood, 17
first aid, pet care, 148
fish:
    in diet, 91, 95
    feeding pets, 145
flame-retardants, synthetic
    fabrics, 41
flavourings, food additives, 97, 187
flax insulation, 24
fleas, 143, 146–7, 149
flies, 61, 150
floors:
    carpets, 42–3
    cleaning, 51, 52
    hard floors, 43
    home offices, 154
    insulation, 25
fluorescent light bulbs, 21, 155
fluoridation, water supply, 98, 187
foamed glass insulation, 24
foil, reusing, 87
food, 89–109
    additives, 96–7, 137
    for babies and young children,
    136–7
    cooking, 109
    drinks, 98–9
    genetically modified (GM)
    foods, 97
    growing your own, 104–5
    improving skin condition, 115
    irradiation, 96
    labels, 96–7, 101
    leftovers, 107
    nutrition, 90–1
    organic food, 92–5, 100–1
    packaging, 102
    pet care, 144–5, 150
    preparation, 106–7
    shopping, 100–3
    storing, 108
    wild foods, 103
"food combining", 91
food stains, removing, 67–8, 137
foot care, 123
formaldehyde, 187
    cleaning materials, 48
    in cosmetics, 113
    in nail varnish, 122
    residues in food, 93
    in shampoos, 120

in synthetic fabrics, 40, 41
in timber products, 13
foundation, 115
fragrances, 188
in cosmetics, 124–5
in the home, 49
free-range chicken, 95
freezers, 27, 103
bulk-cooking, 109
food hygiene, 107
fridges, 27
cleaning, 53
food hygiene, 107
power cuts, 109
recycling, 80
fruit, 90
buying in season, 101
chemical residues, 93–4
"food combining", 91
food hygiene, 107
organic food, 92, 100–1
fruit juices, 137
fruit stains, removing, 68
"full-spectrum" light bulbs, 21
furniture:
cleaning, 56–7
home offices, 155, 159
recycling, 80

G
garages, 10
gardens:
compost, 82–3
growing vegetables, 104–5
water conservation, 15
garlic:
natural remedies, 131
for pets, 145, 147
gas supply, 10, 17
genetically modified (GM) foods, 97
Giardia, 98
gilt, cleaning, 59
ginger ale, 129
glass:
cleaning glassware, 59
cleaning windows, 50
recycling, 79, 87
repairs, 87
global warming, 19

glue, 87
removing, 69
glycerine, 66, 114, 116
glyceryl stearate, 114
gold leaf, cleaning, 59
grapefruit seed extract, 47
grass stains, removing, 68, 69
grease stains, removing, 51, 52, 68–9
green clay masks, skin care, 116
green tea, 99
Greenpeace, 161
greetings cards, reusing, 86
grilling food, 109
guinea pigs, 147, 151

H
hair care, 120–1
hair sprays, 16, 121
halogen light bulbs, 21
hamsters, 151
hand care, 122
handkerchiefs, laundry, 65, 69
handwashing, 71
hangovers, 129
hardwoods, 12
Hay diet, 91
hazardous wastes, 84–5
head lice, 120
headaches, natural remedies, 129
headphones, 27
health care:
natural remedies, 127–33
pets, 148–9
heartburn, 130
heating:
air pollution, 17
energy conservation, 22–3
home offices, 155
hemp:
insulation, 24
matting, 43
soft furnishings, 38
henna, 121
heptachlor expoxide, 93
herbalism, 127, 130–1
herbicides, disposal of, 85
hessian, 38
hexane, 99
hi-fi units, 27

home offices, 153–9
homeopathy, 127, 144, 148
hookworms, 150
hops, natural remedies, 131
hormones, residues in food, 94–5
hot water tanks, 22, 23, 25
house plants, 17
houses, building materials, 10–13
human rights, fair trade, 160
humidity, 17
hydrogenated oils, 91
hydrosols, 146
hygiene:
kitchens, 106–7
pets, 150–1
hypericum:
natural remedies, 131

I
immune system, 136, 137, 145, 148
incandescent light bulbs, 20
indigestion, 130
inks, printing, 155
insecticides, 60
air pollution, 16
disposal of, 85
residues in food, 93–4
timber treatments, 13
insects:
bites and stings, 129
household pests, 60–1
insulation, 10–11, 22, 24–5
insurance, ethical, 161
investment, ethical, 160–1
ionizers, 17, 155
ironing, 36, 37, 73
de–calcifying irons, 73
scorch marks, 69
ironwork, cleaning, 57
irradiated food, 96
isopropyl alcohol, 66

J
jewellery, cleaning, 58
junk mail, 157
jute:
matting, 43
soft furnishings, 38

K

K-sorbate, 114
kathon GC, 113
kettles, 26, 53, 109
keyboards, computers, 156, 158, 159
kitchens:
    appliances, 26–7
    cleaning, 52–3
    hygiene, 106–7
    water conservation, 14
knives, cleaning, 57

L

labels:
    cosmetics, 112–13
    food, 96–7, 101
    washing instructions, 64
lacquer, cleaning, 59
landfill sites, 76
lanolin, 113, 116
laser printers, 155, 157
laundry, 63–73
laundry balls, 70
lavender, natural remedies, 131
lead, pollution, 10
lead-soldered cans, 102
leaf mould, 83, 104
lemon hair spray, 121
lemon juice, 47
lice, 120
lighting:
    energy conservation, 20–1
    home offices, 155, 158
    light bulbs, 20–1, 77, 155
limescale, 54
limewash paint, 33, 34
lindane, 13, 93, 113, 188
linen, soft furnishings, 36
linoleic acid, 91
linoleum, 43, 51
linseed oil, 51
lipstick, 115
    stain removal, 68–9
litter trays, hygiene, 150
loft insulation, 22, 24–5
longlife products, waste
    reduction, 77

M

magazines, recycling, 78
make-up, 115
maleic hydrazide, 93
manufactured mineral fibres
    (MMFs), insulation, 25
marble, cleaning, 51, 55
mascara, 115
masks, skin care, 116
massage, 127
massage oils, 124
mattresses, 38, 39
    cots, 140–1
MEA (monoethanolamine), 112
meadowsweet, natural remedies, 131
meal planning, 91
meat:
    cooking, 107
    feeding pets, 144, 145
    organic meat, 94–5
medicines:
    disposal of, 85
    natural remedies, 127–33
meditation, 127, 132, 133
melamine, 13, 188
metals:
    cleaning, 57–9
    recycling, 79
    in water supply, 98
methanol, 66
methomyl, 93
methylated spirits, 34, 66
methylene chloride, 35, 99
methylmercury, 95
methylparaben, 113
mice, 60
microbes, in water supply, 98
microwave ovens, 27, 53, 109
mildew, cleaning, 55
milk:
    bottle feeding, 136
    pollution, 94–5
milk paint, 33
mineral fibre insulation, 24
mineral oils, 112, 115
minerals, in diet, 90
mobile phones:
    recycling, 80
    safety, 27

transmitters, 10
moisturizers, 116, 119, 123
money, 160–1
mortgages, 161
mosquitoes, 61
mother-of-pearl, cleaning, 59
moths, 37, 42, 60
motor oil, disposal of, 84–5
mould, cleaning, 55
mouse mats, 156
mouthwashes, 119
MSG (monosodium glutamate), 97
mulches, 83
mushrooms, 103

N

nail polish, 85, 122
naphthalene, 50, 60, 188
nappies, 138–9
nappy rash, 138, 139
natural light, 20
natural remedies, 127–33
nausea, 129
neem, natural remedies, 131
negative ions, 17, 158
newspapers, recycling, 78
nitrates, 188
    food additives, 97
    in water supply, 98
nitrites, food additives, 97
NTA, 71, 188
nutrition, 90–1
nylon, soft furnishings, 40

O

octyl dimethyl PABA, 113
octyl methoxycinnamate, 113
odours:
    air fresheners, 16, 49, 124
    pet hygiene, 151
offices, home, 153–9
oil-based paints, 32, 69
oils:
    cooking oils, 91
    disposal of, 84–5
    skin care, 116
    stain removal, 68, 69
    see also essential oils
omega-3 fatty acids, 91, 145

omega-6 fatty acids, 91, 145
optical brighteners, washing
    powders, 70, 188
oral care, 119, 137
organic food, 92–5, 100–1
organic wines and beer, 102
organophosphates (OPS), 93
oryzanol, 117
osteopathy, 127
ovens, 53, 109
ozone, air quality, 32, 154
ozone layer, 16, 189

P

packaging:
    food, 102
    recycling, 81
    waste reduction, 76–7
paints:
    cleaning paintwork, 50
    disposal of, 34, 85
    natural paints, 31, 33–4
    stain removal, 69
    toxic ingredients, 32
paper:
    home offices, 157
    insulation, 24
    recycling, 78, 86
parabens, 113
paraffin, 112
paraffin wax, 93
parasites:
    pets, 150, 151
    in water supply, 98
parathion-methyl, 93
PCBs, 136, 190
PCP (pentachlorophenol), 13
pennyroyal, 147
PERC (perchloroethylene), 50, 73,
    189
percarbonate, 71, 189
perfume, 124–5
perlite, 24
permethrin, 13, 42, 146, 189
personal care, 111–25
persulphate salts, 113
pesticides, 136, 146, 92, 93–4,
    102
pests:
    crop rotation, 105

household pests, 60–1
    on pets, 143, 146–7
petrochemicals, 189
    in cosmetics, 111, 112
    in fragrances, 124
    synthetic fabrics, 40
petrol, 10, 28, 29
petrolatum, 112
pets, 143–51
    feeding, 144–5
    health care, 148–9
    hygiene, 106, 150–1
    pest control, 143, 146–7
    stain removal, 51
pewter, cleaning, 57
phenol, 122, 189
phosphates, 48, 189
photocopiers, 155, 156
phthalates, 43, 141, 189
Pilates, 127
pillow slips, 38, 39, 141
pillows, 38
plants:
    air quality, 17
    compost, 82–3
plastic wrap, 108
plastics, 190
    food packaging, 102
    food storage, 108
    recycling, 78–9
    reusing, 87
    toys, 141
polishes:
    beeswax, 56, 57
    cleaning cars, 29
    disposal of, 85
    synthetic, 56
pollution:
    air, 10, 16–17
    and children, 135
    in fish, 95
    water, 98
polycarbonate, 108
polyester, soft furnishings, 40, 41
polystyrene, 190
    recycling, 78
positive ions, 17, 158
pot-pourri, 49
potassium sorbate, 114
pots and pans:
    cleaning, 52

cooking methods, 109
    energy conservation, 109
    safety, 107
poultry,
    bacterial contamination, 95
power cuts, freezers, 109
power lines, 10
PPD (paraphenylene–diamine),
    112
pre–soaking laundry, 64
pre–wash cleaner, 65
pregnancy:
    herbal treatments, 130
    pet hygiene, 150, 151
pressed–wood products, 11
printers, 81, 156
printing inks, 155
probiotics, 91
processed foods, 91, 92
propxur, 146
propylene glycol, 112
propylparaben, 113
protein, 90
    "food combining", 91
    stain removal, 67
pumice stone, 123
puppies, 151
PVC (polyvinyl chloride), 13, 190
    flooring, 43
    insulation, 25
    soft furnishings, 40
    toys, 141
pyrethroid, 13

R

rabbits, flea control, 147
radiation, working at a computer,
    158
radiators, 23
radio, 27
radon, 10, 190
rags, 47
rainwater, 15
ramie, soft furnishings, 38
rats, 60
rattan furniture, cleaning, 56
rayon, 40, 119
recycling, 11, 75–87
red wine stains, removing, 68

refrigerators see fridges
resorsinol, 120
reverse osmosis water filters, 99
rockwool, insulation, 25
rose water, as skin toner, 116
roundworms, 150
RSI (repetitive strain injury), 158, 159
rubbish, recycling, 75–87
rugs, 43
rust:
    cleaning ironwork, 57
    stain removal, 69

S

sage oil, 47
salads, 91, 109
salmon, fish farming, 95
salmonella, 95
salt, 47, 115
sanitary pads, 119
saturated fats, 91
saucepans see pots and pans
scorch marks, removing, 69
scourers, 47
scratches, on furniture, 56
seagrass matting, 43
seasonal fruits and vegetables, 101
seaweed supplements, 145
selenium sulphide, 120
shampoos, 120
    baby care, 139
    chemicals, 112, 113
    pet care, 149
    soapwort shampoo, 120
shaving, 125
sheep's wool felt insulation, 24
sheets, 38, 39, 72, 141
shellac, 13, 93
shellfish, 95
shoe polish stains, 69
shoes, 77, 80
shopping:
    car travel, 28
    food, 100–3
    waste reduction, 76–7
shower curtains, 54
showers, 15, 54
"sick building syndrome", 9
silk, soft furnishings, 38

silver, cleaning, 58
sinks, 52, 106
sisal matting, 43
skin cancer, 117
skin care, 114–17
    babies, 139
    foot care, 123
    hand care, 122
    pets, 149
skylights, 20, 155
sleep, 115
slippery elm, natural remedies, 131
smog, 32
smoke detectors, disposal of, 85
smoking, 115
soap, 47, 48, 118, 139
soapwort shampoo, 120
sodium benzoate, 114
sodium hypochlorite, 66
sodium lauryl sulphate (SLS), 112, 120
"soft chemistry" cleaning products, 46
soft furnishings, 36–41, 80
softwoods, 12–13
soil:
    growing vegetables, 104
    mulches, 83
    organic food, 92
solar heating, 23
solvents, wallpaper strippers, 35
sore throat, 129
spectacle lenses, recycling, 87
sponges, 47
spot removers, 66
stain removers, 66–9, 137
starches, "food combining", 91
stationery, 157
steam facials, 116
steaming food, 109
stearic acid, 114
steel:
    cleaning, 57
    recycling, 79
stings, insect, 129
stomach problems, 129
stone, cleaning, 51
storage:
    food, 108
    home offices, 154

stress relief, working at home, 153
strippers, wallpaper, 35
styrene, 42, 43, 191
sucralose, 91
sugar, 90, 137
sulphates, 48, 191
sulphites, 97, 102
sunburn, 117
sunflower oil, 145
sunlight, 20, 117
sunscreens, 113, 117
supermarkets, 100–1
surface cleaner, 53
sweat stains, 69
sweeteners, artificial, 91
synthetic fabrics, soft furnishings, 40–1
synthetic organic chemicals, 93, 98

T

T'ai Chi, 127
talcum powder, 123, 139
tampons, 119
tapeworms, 150, 151
taps, cleaning, 54
tar stains, removing, 69
TBTO (tributyltin oxide), 13
tea, 99
    hair rinse, 121
    stain removal, 52, 68
tea tree oil, 47, 131, 147
TEA (triethanolamine), 112
teeth, 15, 137
telephones, 154, 156, 80
    see also mobile phones
television, 26, 27
terracotta tiles, cleaning, 51
textiles:
    furnishings, 31
    laundry, 63–73
    moths, 60
    recycling, 80, 87
    soft furnishings, 36–41
    stain removers, 66–9
thermostats, 23
throat problems, 129
thyme oil, 47, 131
ticks, 143, 147
tiles, cleaning, 51

tissues, 119
tocopherol, 114
toilet cleaners, 48
toilet tissues, 119
toiletries see cosmetics
toilets, 15, 55
toluene, 98, 122, 191
toner cartridges, 81, 156
tooth care, 15, 137
toothpaste, 112, 113, 119
towels, 31
Toxic Shock Syndrome, 119
toxocariasis, 150, 151
toxoplasmosis, 150, 151
toys, 80, 141
Traidcraft, 160
trans-fats, 91
travel, energy conservation, 28–9
trichloroethane
   perchloroethylene, 66
triclosan, 125
trihalomethanes, 98
TRIS, 41
trout, fish farming, 95
tumble-dryers, 72
tuolene, 42
turpentine, 34, 66, 191

U

ultra-violet rays, 20
   sunscreens, 113, 117
upholstery, 31
   stain removal, 68
urine, pet hygiene, 151

V

vaccinations, pet care, 148
valerian, natural remedies, 131
varnish, shellac, 13
vases, cleaning, 59
VDUs, 158
vegetables, 90
   buying in season, 101
   chemical residues, 93–4
   "food combining", 91
   food hygiene, 107
   growing your own, 104–5
   organic food, 92, 100–1
ventilation, 16, 17, 155

vermiculite, 24, 191
vets, 148
video recorders, 26, 27
vinegar, 47
   cider vinegar, 116, 147
   cleaning appliances, 53
   cleaning bathrooms, 54, 55
   cleaning tiles, 51
   cleaning windows, 50
   stripping wallpaper, 35
vinyl chloride, 98
vinyl paints, 32
viscose rayon, 40, 119
vitamins, 90
   supplements for pets, 145
   vitamin C, 117
   vitamin E, 114, 116, 117
volatile organic compounds
   (VOCs), 32, 42, 98

W

wallpaper, 35, 50
walls:
   cleaning, 50
   insulation, 25
washing, 63–73
   bedding, 39
   drying and pressing, 72–3
   laundry, 64–5, 70–1
   natural fabrics, 36–8
   stain removers, 66–9
   synthetic fabrics, 41
washing machines, 64, 65
   calcium deposits, 71
   cleaning, 53
   energy conservation, 26
   water conservation, 14
washing powder, 70, 71
washing soda, 47, 66
washing up liquid, 48
waste:
   recycling, 75–87
   reducing, 76–7
water:
   cleaning with, 45
   conservation, 14–15, 26
   drinking, 77, 98–9
   stain removal with, 67
   treatment plants, 15
   water heaters, 14

water softeners, 52
watermarks, on furniture, 56
wax:
   emulsifying wax, 114
   food coatings, 93
   removing from candlesticks, 59
   stain removal, 68
wheatgerm oil, 145
white spirit, 34, 66, 191
wild foods, 103
willow, natural remedies, 131
windows:
   cleaning, 50
   draughtproofing, 25
   home offices, 155
   natural light, 20
   secondary glazing, 22
wine, 102
   stain removal, 68
witch hazel, 125, 131
wood, 12–13
   chopping boards, 52
   fires, 17
   floors, 43, 51
   furniture, 56
   pressed–wood products, 11
   recycling, 81
   wood fibreboard insulation, 24
wool:
   bedding, 38
   carpets, 42, 43
   soft furnishings, 37
work surfaces, 52, 53, 107
working at home, 153–9
worms, pets, 150, 151
wormwood, 147
wrapping paper, reusing, 86

X

Xenex, 147
xylene, 42, 122, 191

Y

yoga, 127, 132–3, 159
yogurt, as skin cleanser, 116

Z

zeolite, 71

GLOSSARY

AEROSOL PROPELLANTS

Contain liquified toxic gases and are present in personal care items and household aerosol products. Typical propellants include liquified petroleum gas (LPG), used in household aerosol products, and dimethyl ether, common in personal care products. The gases may penetrate lungs and skin more easily than those distributed by pump-action sprays, because the dispersion is finer and more easily absorbed by the lungs and skin. CFC liquified aerosol propellant gases are no longer used in aerosols in the West, but they are permitted in inhalation aerosols used in the treatment of asthma (see also CFCs). They may cause headaches, nausea, dizziness, eye and throat irritation or injury, skin rashes, heart problems, birth defects, and lung cancer,

ACETONE

A manufactured chemical also found naturally in the environment, acetone is a flammable, colourless liquid with a distinct smell and taste. Used to make nail polish, paint, and household chemicals; it is also found in plastics, fibres, and drugs, and is present in vehicle exhaust fumes, tobacco smoke, and landfill sites. Harmless in small doses, but over-exposure by touching or breathing in acetone can cause nose, lung, throat, and eye irritation, and shortening of the female menstrual cycle.

AMMONIA

A natural gas with a sharp odour that is soluble in water, and the only volatile alkali on earth. Household products containing ammonia should be used sparingly and with caution since exposure to ammonia can cause eye irritation and conjunctivitis, respiratory tract problems, and skin burn. About 80 per cent of the ammonia that is made in factories is used to make fertilizers. The remaining 20 per cent is used in textiles, plastics, explosives, pulp and paper production, household cleaning products, and refrigerants.

ASBESTOS

A mineral that is resistant to heat, fire, and corrosive chemicals. If its micro-porous fibres are inhaled, they can cause chronic lung disease (asbestosis) and cancer (mesothelioma). Generally, material in good condition will not release asbestos fibres. There is no danger unless fibres are worn or damaged. Until the 1970s, many types of building products and insulation materials used in homes contained asbestos. It was found in roofing shingles, insulation, plasterboard, floor and ceiling tiles, heating pipes, and ventilation ducts. It was also used to make fire-resistant household products, such as oven gloves and ironing-board covers. Most products made today do not contain asbestos. Those few products that are still made with asbestos are required to be labelled as such.

BENZENE

A colourless liquid with a sweet odour. It is highly flammable and is formed from both natural processes and human activities. Indoor air generally contains higher levels of benzene from products that contain it, such as glues, paints, furniture wax, and detergents. Natural sources of benzene include volcanoes and forest fires. Benzene is also a natural part of crude oil, gasoline, and cigarette smoke. It is carcinogenic and a central nervous system depressant. It may cause light-headedness, a staggering gait, disorientation, fatigue, loss of appetite, skin and lung irritation, anaemia, reproductive problems, leukaemia, and myeloma.

BORAX

Borax, or sodium tetraborate, is a naturally occurring mineral. It is a colourless, crystalline salt; it also occurs as a white powder. Borax is widely and diversely used, for example, as a mild antiseptic, a cleansing agent, a water softener, and in the manufacture of enamels, shellacs, heat-resistant glass, fertilizers, pharmaceuticals, and other chemicals. It contains the element boron (see below).

BORON

A mineral element that is a necessary food supplement for some living creatures, but can be damaging at high levels. Pure boron is a little-used dark powder, but boron compounds are important in many industries, such as glass and detergent manufacture and agriculture. Boron compounds are used in fertilizers to aid in plant growth and yield. Boron is an essential mineral for plants but not animals – in fact, it can be toxic in excess.

CFCS

Chlorofluorocarbons, or CFCs, are used as liquified gas propellants in aerosol cans, in the blowing of polystyrene packaging, in the refrigerants that remove heat from fridges and freezers (which accounts for one-quarter of all CFCs), in car seats and foam mattresses, in dry cleaning, and fire extinguishers. They have been linked to the deterioration of the ozone layer and act as a "greenhouse gas", adding to global warming.

CHLORINE

A heavy yellowish-green gas with a powerful odour, used as a bleaching and disinfectant agent. It was used during World War I as a chemical weapon. Chlorine penetrates the skin and can aggravate sensitive areas in the eyes, nose, throat, and lungs, and has been linked with high blood pressure, diabetes, and heart disease. Chlorine bleaching of paper and other items creates polychlorinated biphenyls (PCBs), which are known to cause sterility and cancer.

COLOURS

FD&C colours (used in food, drugs, and cosmetics) are made from coal tar, and tests on animals show them to be carcinogenic. They may cause hyperactivity, eczema, asthma, behavioural disturbances in children, dizziness, headaches, mental confusion, skin rashes, and gastritis.

DIOXINS

A group of chemical compounds, some of which are produced by the chlorine bleaching of wood pulp and other industrial processes, including the incineration of waste. The term dioxin is sometimes used to refer to one of the most toxic dioxins, 2,3,7,8-tetrachlorodibenzo-p-dioxin (TCDD), considered by scientists to be the most potent synthetic poison ever created. Exposure to large amounts of dioxins may result in skin diseases and liver damage. Dioxins may cause mutagenic effects on foetal development, and have been linked to cancer. Dioxins find their way up the food chain, and human exposure may come from milk, butter, meat, poultry, and fish that contain traces of dioxins.

EDTA

This widely used water-softener is processed from crude oil. It may damage the environment, and pose a hazard to drinking water.

ENZYMES

Natural catalysts obtained, in the case of washing powders, from bacteria and used to break down protein stains. Their action on human proteins may produce skin problems and respiratory complaints: enzymes are considered a factor in the growing incidence of allergic reactions.

ETHANOL

The type of alcohol that is present in wines and beers when fermented from sugars. Much ethanol – not intended for drinking – is now made synthetically from ethylene, derived from petroleum. This type of ethanol is used as an automotive fuel by itself and can be mixed with gasoline. Ethanol may cause depression of the central nervous system, anaesthesia, impaired motor co-ordination, double vision, and nausea.

FLAVOURS

Around 1,500 petrochemical derivatives are used as flavourings in food. They can cause hyperactivity and behavioural disorders.

FLUORIDE

Although this mineral occurs naturally in water, some countries add fluoride to the water supply as a treatment chemical to prevent tooth decay. It is also present in most toothpastes. However, a growing number of scientists now question the value of supplementing fluoride intake, even in small amounts. Some studies indicate that fluoridation does not improve dental health. In addition, low levels of exposure to fluoride may lead to tiredness; weakness; kidney, bladder, and stomach disorders; eczema; and a weak immune system. Its use in the water supply is banned in many European countries.

FORMALDEHYDE

A colourless gas with a pungent odour used as a preservative, bonding agent, and fire retardant. A suspected human carcinogen and mutagenic agent, it has been shown to cause cancer in animals. Formaldehyde may be a contributing factor to Sudden Infant Death Syndrome (cot death). Exposure may cause coughs, throat problems, eye irritation, respiratory problems, headaches, rashes, tiredness, nausea, and insomnia. Long term exposure may lead to allergic sensitization. Formaldehyde may be found in carpets, fabrics, permanent-press clothes, particle board and pressed-wood products, paints, lipstick, toothpaste, shampoo, grocery bags, paper towels, facial tissues, and soft drinks, among other items. Formaldehyde may continue to "off-gas" for up to seven to eight years.

FRAGRANCES

Many synthetic fragrances used to scent personal care and household products may contain as many as 4,000 separate, unlisted ingredients. Exposure to synthetic fragrances can cause headaches, dizziness, skin discoloration, skin irritation, coughing, vomiting, and behavioural problems.

HARD CHEMISTRY

In the process of "hard" as opposed to "soft chemistry", raw materials, such as crude oil – an unrenewable resource – are unravelled into their basic structure of atoms and molecules and then rebuilt. This process is energy-intensive and polluting, often releasing dangerous by-products into the environment.

LINDANE

An extremely toxic organo-chlorine insecticide that is easily absorbed by the skin. It is used as a seed and wood treatment, an insecticidal spray for a range of food crops, a veterinary insecticide on livestock and pets, and the active ingredient in head lice shampoos and in lotions to treat scabies. Exposure may cause convulsion and seizures, and cancers in laboratory animals. It is a possible human carcinogen, and it has been linked to breast cancer. Lindane is being phased out for use in farming in the European Union, and it is banned in some countries in other parts of the world.

MELAMINE

A thermoplastic polymer of methylene and dimethylene ether based on petrochemicals whose manufacture is polluting. It is resistant to heat, flame, and solvents. Melamine is used in fire-blocking fabrics, aircraft seating, protective clothing, thermal liners, air filters, and as a veneer on particle board for kitchen fittings. If particles of melamine become airborne – for example, when melamine board is sawn – they may cause irritation to the respiratory tract.

NAPHTHALENE

This volatile liquid is distilled from petrochemicals, and is a constituent of bitumen and asphalt. It is also found in some air fresheners and fragrances. Napthalene is a suspected human carcinogen. It may cause skin irritation, headaches, confusion, nausea and vomiting, and sweating.

NITRATES

Naturally occurring and harmless in themselves, nitrates can be turned to nitrites in the body, where they lower blood pressure and may cause headaches, vertigo, and palpitations. Nitrates are present in most waterways because they wash off agricultural land, where they are used as a fertilizer.

NTA

Nitrilotriacetic acid (NTA) is an environmentally polluting water-softener derived from crude oil. It is widely used as a phosphate replacement in dishwasher detergents and washing powders.

OPTICAL BRIGHTENERS

These styrol derivatives are added to washing agents to convert UV light into visible light and so make washing lighter and brighter. Their chemical structure makes them allergenic and they are suspected carcinogens.

ORGANOCHLORINES

A family of chemical compounds produced by combining chlorine with organic substances, usually petrochemicals. While many are produced commercially, some occur as unwanted by-products in industrial processes. Organochlorines include dioxins, heptachlor, PCBs, lindane, DDT, dieldrin, aldrin, hexachlorobenzene, and pentachlorophenol. Organochlorines may be used in plastics, paints, dyes, pesticides, deodorants, bleaching agents, refrigerants, wood preservers, and cleaning solvents. Organochlorines may be connected to oestrogen-related cancers in women, and they have a severe negative impact on the environment.

OZONE

Ozone is a gas consisting of three oxygen molecules. A layer of ozone protects the earth from UV rays from the sun. At ground level, however, it is a pollutant and contributes to city smog in hot weather. Ozone is vulnerable to gases containing chlorine, such as CFCs (chlorofluorocarbons), which have destroyed parts of the protective ozone layer.

PARADICHLOROBENZENE

This is a white solid crystal with an oily surface. It has a moth-ball-like odour. Paradichlorobenzene may be found in toilet-bowl deodorizers, air fresheners, and moth balls. It is listed as a poison. Inhalation may cause headaches, and skin, throat, and eye irritation, and ingestion can cause damage to kidneys and liver.

PERBORATE

Sodium perborate tetrahydrate is a white crystalline powder made of sodium borate and hydrogen peroxide. It is the most widely used bleaching agent in washing powders, and may release damaging amounts of boron.

PERCARBONATE

Sodium percarbonate is the most eco-friendly stain remover and bleaching agent except for sunlight. It creates no environmental hazards. It is used in laundry products.

PERCHLOROETHYLENE

This liquid chemical solvent is used to remove stains and soiling from clothing in the dry-cleaning process. Highly toxic, it is flagged as a possible human carcinogen (perchloroethylene causes cancer in rats). It may cause headaches, giddiness, nausea, and eye and skin irritation, and high levels of exposure have been linked with damage to the liver and central nervous system. It is suspected of causing birth defects in people who have long-term exposure to perchloroethylene.

PERMETHRIN

An odourless concentrate used as an insecticide and repellent. It is a synthetic version of naturally occurring pyrethrin found in flowers. Permethrin is long-lasting as an insect repellent on clothing fibres, but it is less effective when applied directly to the skin. Although it is generally considered safer than some types of insecticide, there is still concern as to its safety.

PETROCHEMICALS

These are all derivatives of petrochemicals, including mineral oils, petroleum, paraffin, and any compound ending in -ethyl or -enzene. They come from non-renewable resources, and their manufacture is polluting to the environment. Many petrochemicals have toxic side effects, some of them severe (even small doses of paraffin may cause cancer in mice). Petrochemicals are widely used in many household and cosmetic products.

PH VALUE

Measure of acidity or alkalinity of a solution.

PHENOLS

These derivatives of benzene are known to be toxic and they may be carcinogenic. High exposure may cause nausea, skin rashes, and respiratory problems. Phenols are present in synthetic resins in hard plastics, paints, coatings and varnishes, fungicides, and wood preservatives.

PHOSPHATES

These salts of phosphoric acid are used as water softeners. Phosphates are recognized as being environmentally damaging because they may cause eutrophication (encouraging algae to grow faster in water systems, thereby upsetting the natural ecological balance).

PHTHALATES

Chemicals used as plasticizers. These compounds are found in PVC, for example in medical plastic tubing and PVC toys for babies and children, and in a range of personal care products, such as shampoos, hair conditioners, moisturizers, soaps, perfumes, hair sprays, and nail polish. Plasticizers do not bind to PVC and can leach out. The plasticizer DEHA, for example, is used in some food wraps and containers, and may migrate into foods that have a high fat content. Other phthalates used in food packaging may leach into food if exposed to conditions warmer than room temperature. The most widely used phthalate is diethylhexyl phthalate (DEHP). Animal studies indicate that large amounts of DEHP may disrupt normal hormone function and cause birth defects. The US Environmental Protection Agency considers DEHP to be a probable carcinogen. The European Union has banned the use of certain phthalates in toys for infants. In the US, the use of phthalates is also limited in baby pacifiers and teethers.

PLASTICS
Plastics cause problems because they may "off-gas", especially when heated. Many of these fumes are suspected human carcinogens: those from epoxy resin, acrylonitrile, polyethelene, PVC, and polyester may cause lung and skin disorders. Inhaling PVP (polyvinylpyrrolidone) can cause cancer in animals.

POLYSTYRENE
This is a petroleum by-product (a long chain of styrene molecules joined together) and is used to make egg cartons, coffee cups, and packing materials. Polystyrene is polluting in manufacture and is not biodegradable.

PCBS
Polychlorinated biphenyls are an extremely toxic group of chemicals that were once widely used as a non-flammable oil in electrical equipment, fluorescent light ballasts, hydraulic fluids, waterproof wall coverings, adhesives, textile treatments, wrapping papers, fire retardants, brake linings, plastics, and paints. Although the use of PCBS has been phased out in many countries, they are very persistent and remain in the environment for many years. For example, minute traces of PCBs may be found in numerous foods, especially fatty foods. Exposure may cause a severe skin rash, liver damage, a respiratory disorder, thyroid gland imbalance, muscle and joint pain, and headaches. PCBs are a proven animal carcinogen and suspected of causing cancer in humans.

PVC
Polyvinyl chloride (PVC), also known as vinyl, is a chlorinated plastic and one of the most widely used plastics. It may also be one of the most environmentally damaging. PVC manufacture uses large amounts of chlorine, and this process creates polluting waste. Untreated, PVC is a rigid plastic; to make it soft or flexible, plasticizers known as phthalates are added. These ingredients are not chemically bound to the PVC, and can migrate out via moisture, evaporation, or contact with other materials. Metal salts, such as lead, zinc, and organic tin compounds, may be added as stabilizers in PVC; unfortunately, these may also leach out of the PVC. Vinyl chloride, a mildly sweet-smelling gas used in the manufacture of PVC, may "off-gas" from certain PVC materials, especially when new – for example, the plastic parts in a new car may give off vinyl chloride vapours. (Vinyl chloride is also present in tobacco smoke.) Workers exposed to vinyl chloride have reported symptoms such as dizziness, nausea, stomach pain, breathlessness, and circulatory problems. It has been linked to liver and spleen damage, it is mutagenic in humans, and is possibly carcinogenic. PVC is difficult to recycle, so it is either incinerated, which releases dioxins and other toxic chemicals, and leaves behind toxic ash, or it is disposed of in landfill sites, where chemicals may leach into the soil and ground water. PVC is used to make window frames, wood mouldings, pipes, vinyl flooring, wallpaper, toys, adhesives, shower curtains, clothes, food packaging, plastic wrap, and furniture.

RADON GAS
A naturally occurring, radioactive, colourless, odourless gas that is the second-highest cause of lung cancer after smoking. In areas where radon gas is present, sometimes house construction methods can release the gas, so levels may be tested by the environmental health office.

SODIUM HYDROXIDE
Also known as caustic soda.

SOFT CHEMISTRY
This term is used to describe chemical products that are based on ingredients that come from natural sources and that are renewable. Soft chemistry uses raw materials such as coconut, sugar cane, lemon, and spices. Common minerals, such as sand, chalk, lime, and silicates, are also used, since they are present in large

quantities in nature and find their way back into the environment without damaging it. The ultimate aim of soft chemistry is to interfere as little as possible with the raw materials to avoid polluting manufacturing processes.

STYRENE

This is a synthetic chemical that is also known as vinylbenzene, ethenylbenzene, or phenylethelene. A colourless liquid with a sweet smell, it evaporates easily and is used in the manufacture of building materials, carpet backing, resins, rubber, plastic, insulation, fibreglass, pipes, and food containers. Styrene vapours are acutely irritating to the skin, eyes, and upper respiratory tract, and they may also affect the gastrointestinal system. Chronic exposure to styrene vapours may affect the central nervous system, causing depression, fatigue headaches, weakness, and minor kidney problems. It is a suspected human carcinogen.

SULPHATES

The filler that makes a concentrated washing powder a non-concentrated powder, but has no effect on the washing action and is a burden on the environment.

SYNTHETIC

"Hard chemistry" cleaning agents that contain surfactants (surface active agents) based on petrochemicals that separate fats and oils and keep the oil droplets suspended in water. They may cause dermatitis, flu- and asthma-like symptoms, severe eye damage, and

respiratory tract injury if ingested. They may cause environmental pollution.

TOLUENE

A preservative and bonding agent used in cosmetic polishes, such as nail varnish, and many household and building materials. A suspected human carcinogen, prolonged exposure can cause liver and kidney damage, dermatitis, birth defects, miscarriage, headaches, nausea, and asthma.

TURPENTINE

This natural yellow to brown oleoresin (a semisolid mixture of a resin and essential oil) seeps out of the bark of sapwood pines, firs, and other conifers. Turpentine production is environmentally friendly, since trees are encouraged to grow to maturity and beyond.

VERMICULITE

A natural mica-like mineral based on silicates of aluminium and magnesium. Used in insulation, packaging, filler and lightweight concrete, and as a bedding medium for young plants.

VINYL

Otherwise known as polyvinyl chloride (PVC), vinyl is a thermoplastic that was originally developed in the 1920s as a substitute for rubber, with inherent flame-retardant properties. Vinyl is made by converting basic petrochemicals (petroleum, natural gas, or coal), with the addition of chlorine, chemical additives, and modifiers.

It is ubiquitous, environmentally polluting, and can be a hazard to human health.

WHITE SPIRIT

A colourless solvent made of a mixture of mineral salts. Among its many uses, it is a paint thinner and general-purpose grease remover. White spirit can sometimes be used instead of turpentine and is much cheaper. Flammable and toxic, it dries out the skin's natural oils and may cause an allergy. It may also be a central nervous system depressant, causing headaches, nausea, giddiness, behavioural disorders, nose and respiratory problems, skin cancers, and miscarriages.

XYLENE

A volatile, colourless liquid used in the preparation of artificial dyes. Exposure may cause nausea, vomiting, coughing, hoarseness, headaches, giddiness, and ringing in the ears.

ACKNOWLEDGMENTS

AUTHOR'S ACKNOWLEDGMENTS

My thanks to all the people I contacted in the course of researching this book, for being generous with their time, information, and enthusiasm: in particular, Edward Milford, Walter Grondzik, Chris Bennett, and Peter Malaise.

Huge thanks to the editorial and design teams at Dorling Kindersley, and to Russell Sadur for his beautiful photographs.

PUBLISHER'S ACKNOWLEDGMENTS

The publisher would like to thank the following:
Diana Craig for help with editing, Margherita Gianni for help with design, Hilary Bird for the index. For baby clothes and household textiles: **Greenfibres**, Freepost LON 7805, Totnes, Devon TQ9. Tel: 01803 868 001, www.greenfibres.com.
For cotton and linen fabrics: **Malabar**, 31–32 South Bank Business Centre, Ponton Road, London SW8. Tel: 020 7501 4200, www.malabar.co.uk.
For natural floor coverings and linoleum: **Sinclair Till** 793 Wandsworth Road, London SW8. Tel: 020 7720 0031. For loan of household props: **Jasmine** 65 Abbeville Road, London SW4 Tel: 020 8675 9475 and **Josephine Ryan Antiques**, 63 Abbeville Road, London SW4. Tel: 020 8675 3900.

For wallpapers: **Neisha Crosland wallpapers** available through Paint Library 5, Elystan Street, London SW3. Tel: 020 7823 7755, www.paintlibrary.co.uk. For natural paints: **Francesca Lime Wash Ltd**, Battersea Business Centre, 99–109 Lavender Hill, London SW11. Tel: 020 7228 7694, Email: francesca@ francescapaint. co.uk; **Lakeland Paints**, Unit 34, Heysham Business Park, Middleton Road, Heysham, Lancashire LA3. Tel: 01524 852371, www.ecospaints.com; **Auro Organic Paint Supplies**, Unit 2, Pamphillions Farm, Purton End, Debden, Saffron Walden, Essex CB11. Tel: 01799 543 077, www.auroorganic.co.uk.
For natural insulation materials: **Construction Resources**, 16 Great Guildford Street, London SE1. Tel: 020 7450 2211, www.ecoconstruct.com.

PICTURE CREDITS
Commissioned photography:
Photographer: Russell Sadur
Assistant: Nina Duncan

Other photographs: Peter Anderson: pp.21cr, 28cr; Simon Brown: pp.101cra, 104tr, 104br, 105cr, 135tr, 136cra; John Davis: pp.93tr, 110f, 112cra, bl; 113bl; 115cra, bl, 120clb, 122clb, 124crb; Jake Fitzjones: pp.152f; Craig Knowles: p.82tr; Ian O'Leary: pp.36cra, 77tr, 100tr, 103tr, 109cra, 135cra, 138cl; Reuben Paris: p.19br; Pia Tryde: p.103bl; Colin Walton : p.154cra; Tim Winter : pp.50cra, 60cla, 118cr, 127crb, 130cra. All images © Dorling Kindersley Limited. For further information visit: www.dkimages.com

ILLUSTRATION
Richard Lee: (floorplan) p.154

ABOUT THE AUTHOR

Rosamond Richardson lives in a 17th-century cottage in the English countryside, and has run it along environmental lines since she moved there in 1984. The electricity is generated from renewable sources, she recycles as much waste as possible, and uses organic products. Rosamond has written over 20 books on vegetarian cooking, food from the wild, and country life. Her books on natural health and wellbeing issues are based on her experience as a yoga teacher. Her more recent titles for Kyle Cathie include: *The Great Green Cookbook* (2002), *The Natural Home* (2001), *New Woman: A Survival Guide to Growing Older* (2001), and *Natural Superwoman* (1999).